THE ABC OF ATTRACTING BIRDS

Blue Jays

The ABC of
ATTRACTING
BIRDS

ALVIN M. PETERSON

THE BRUCE PUBLISHING COMPANY
New York   MILWAUKEE   Chicago

1311047

CONTENTS

THE ABC OF ATTRACTING BIRDS

"Robin, Sir Robin, gay, red-vested knight
Now you have come to us, summer's in sight."

Chapter I

SOME REASONS FOR HAVING BIRD NEIGHBORS

DO YOU feel like shouting for joy upon seeing and hearing the first bluebird or robin of spring? Many folks do. The return of the birds tells them that the season of snow and cold is about over, and that soon the days will be long, sunny, and warm, and the hepatica will shortly be peeping from the mold of the forest floor. Spring at last is at hand. Birds, then, are harbingers of spring; they return to us early each year with the message that spring is on the way, thereby adding to our happiness.

1

But what is the first bird to arrive in spring? That depends upon where you live. Many people consider the robin and bluebird to be our harbingers of spring.

> "Robin, Sir Robin, gay, red-vested knight,
>   Now you have come to us, summer's in sight"

sings Lucy Larcom;

> "When bluebirds come the snowy scene
>   Dissolves, as does some golden dream";

writes Nellie Hart Woodworth; and

> "Hark! 'Tis the bluebird's venturesome strain
>   High on the old fringed elm at the gate —
>   . . . .
>   Telling us Spring has come again"

says T. B. Aldrich. And these poets are correct, because the robin and bluebird are two of the first birds to return to many places from their southern winter homes. They are two of the first birds to return where I live, though not always the very first. Sometimes I see them as early as the third and fourth weeks of February, but more often not until the second week in March.

The red-winged blackbird, grackle, killdeer, song sparrow, and meadowlark also return about the time the bluebird and robin make their appearance. Sometimes the killdeer is to be seen a day or two earlier, but more often a day or two later, about the time one hears the first *"chonk-er-ee"* of the redwinged blackbird, the *"Spring-o' the year"* of the

The crow is my harbinger of spring.

meadowlark, the breezy, happy lay of the musical song sparrow, and the creaking notes of grackles.

Nevertheless, the foregoing birds are not the first ones to return where I live, and they are not my harbingers of spring. The honor goes to a large, black bird many people consider a pest, which they kill and persecute for various reasons, and for which they have little sympathy and few kind words — the American crow. It is the first bird to return to this neighborhood from its winter haunts or winter home, and I prize it accordingly and would no more think of killing one than I would think of killing a blue-bird, meadowlark, or robin. I usually see my first crow of the year late in January or early in February, though sometimes it does not return until three or four weeks later.

Most birds are pretty and people enjoy seeing them and observing their bright colors, cunning ways, graceful flight, and interesting habits. Some birds are blue in color, some red, some brown, and others black, orange, yellow, or gray, depending upon the species. However, nearly all of them have their suits brightened and trimmed in some way. The blue jay, for example, besides being blue in color, is brightened with white, and also has a prominent crest and wears a neat, black collar. The bluebird has a reddish breast, the red-winged blackbird orange and red shoulders or epaulets, and the scarlet tanager black wings and tail. The cedar waxwi~ ~ has a yellow bar across the end of the vesper sparrow and slate-colored junco white outer tail feathers, and the chickadee and goldfinch black caps. And none of them fly in exactly the same way. The flicker bounds along, hawks soar, swallows dip and circle, and flycatchers flit and dart. Birds, too, generally are bright-eyed, happy, neat, and full of life. One simply cannot help liking them and wanting them for neighbors.

And how queer some of them act when courting. The ruffed grouse spreads its tail, lowers its wings, and struts much like a turkey gobbler; the same is true of the woodcock and some of the other birds. The flickers are to be seen in pairs, perched on stumps, stubs, and tree trunks, bowing, swinging their heads and breasts from side to side, and uttering notes that sound like *"wick-ie, wick-ie, wick-ie."* The strangest thing about the whole performance is that the two birds usually are "out of step," or out of time, because when one moves its head in one direction, the other moves its in just the opposite.

One of the important reasons why many of us enjoy having birds for neighbors is that we like to listen to their wonderful songs. The catbird, mockingbird, house wren, wood thrush, brown thrasher, rose-breasted grosbeak, orchard oriole, song sparrow, vesper sparrow, and many others are famous songsters. The brown thrasher is one of the most gifted of all our bird songsters, and I like to think of it as being the grand-opera singer of the bird world. It always flies to the top of a tall tree, the top of a telephone pole, or some other prominent place, where it can look out over the world and be seen by its audience to splendid advantage, when it wishes to sing. And then how it does sing, long, loud, clear, and in very rich tones. Its song is varied and consists largely of couplets, a well-known interpretation being:

> *Shuck it, shuck it; sow it, sow it;*
> *Plow it, plow it; hoe it, hoe it!*

The white-throated sparrow is a noted bird songster that has had its song written in many ways, as for example: *"Old Sam Peabody, Peabody, Peabody"*; *"Oh see me me me me me"*; *"Sow wheat, Pev-er-ly, Pev-er-ly, Pev-er-ly"*; and *"Sweet Can-a-da, Can-a-da, Can-a-da."* Albert Field Gilmore tells the story of an old fisherman by the name of Chickering, who heard some of these birds singing when he was lost in the woods. He thought the birds were

Young Bluebirds — Bluebirds are interesting, pretty, and very useful, being bluish above and having reddish breasts, and destroying large numbers of cutworms and grasshoppers.

making fun of him, since they all seemed to be saying:

Poor Mr. — Chickering — Chickering — Chickering
A-l-l night Chickering — Chickering — Chickering.

It is both interesting and instructive to listen to the songs of birds and to try to make out what they are saying and then to write the songs out in words. One that I particularly like to hear because of the queer things it seems to say is the Baltimore oriole. One year all the orioles I saw and heard seemed to be singing, *"Will you really, will you really, really, tru-ly!"*; another year, *"Here, here, here, here. Here, here, here, Pretty"*; and still another, *"Coming over to see you! Coming over to see you!"* Those I have heard the last few years, however, have had the queerest and most appropriate song of all, a good song with plenty of advice for the farmer, singing over and over, *"Potatoes, plant right here. Potatoes, plant right here."*

Moreover, the song of one species of bird differs from that of another, that of the robin being unlike that of the redwing, and that of the orchard oriole differing from that of the rose-breasted grosbeak. The person who is at all attentive to the notes of birds soon learns to identify the common species by their songs alone, and secures a great deal of enjoyment from their music.

From a material standpoint the presence of wild birds is worth much to us in dollars and cents, since they destroy millions upon millions of weed seeds and insects, large numbers of mice, rats, and other rodents, and great quantities of garbage and carrion.

Hawks and owls, birds which are persecuted and killed by many people, are famous for the good work they do in destroying rats and mice, pests that do millions of dollars' worth of damage yearly by entering homes, gnawing holes in floors and walls, digging under buildings, killing poultry, and eating large quantities of food and grain. These birds give the rodents little rest day and night. The rat or mouse that leaves the shelter of its hole by day is likely to be pounced upon by a hawk; and the one that ventures out at night is likely to be caught by an owl.

Scientists working for the United States Department of Agriculture have examined the contents of hundreds of stomachs of hawks and owls and have learned that these birds are our most formidable allies in keeping rats and mice in check. And still many of us kill them whenever we get the chance. Each year rat-exterminating campaigns are conducted in many of our cities and villages, on farms, and about our homes at the cost of thousands of dollars. Much of this expense might be saved had we not killed and almost exterminated hawks and owls, the natural enemies of the pests.

Many birds also are famous as weed-seed destroyers, notably the sparrows, slate-colored junco, goldfinch, mourning dove, meadowlark, bobolink, bobwhite, horned lark, red-winged blackbird, and cardinal. The tree sparrow, goldfinch, and slate-colored junco are among our most famous, eating hundreds and even thousands of tons yearly. They are to be seen all winter long, even in the northern part of the country, frequenting waysides, fence rows, old fields, waste places, gardens, and pastures wherever weeds grow thickly, living on their seeds. Some birds perch on the weeds, peck at their seed heads, dislodge and eat the seeds, while their comrades run over the ground or snow and pick up those to be found there. These birds eat weed seeds throughout the year, but especially during the colder months of the year, when almost all of their food consists of such matter. Though the song, field, chipping, vesper, and some other sparrows winter farther south, much the same may be said in regard to their feeding habits.

The mourning dove spends most of its time in the autumn, winter, and spring in the fields and meadows, picking up, eating, and thus destroying thousands of

Young grackles — "Birds are worth attracting to the premises
in order that they may be studied to better advantage."

weed seeds. Stomach examinations made at Washington, D. C., have shown that this bird is fond of tiny weed seeds, a single bird eating thousands of them in a day. The stomachs of three birds were found to contain more that 23,000 small weed seeds, one holding 7,500 seeds of the yellow wood-sorrel, another 6,400 of those of the foxtail, and the third 9,200 of various noxious plants. Nearly two thirds of this bird's food consists of weed seeds and the rest mainly of waste grain.

More than fifty per cent of the bobwhite's yearly food supply consists of weed seeds; the same is true

of that of the red-winged blackbird. And about one third of the brightly colored cardinal's food supply consists of the same material.

Birds are even more famous and useful for the work they do in destroying insects, some living wholly on small, harmful creatures throughout the year, while others live at least partly on them. Even our most famous weed-seed destroyers do so. And all of them feed insects almost entirely to their young, though some offer their babies berries and other similar foods. Insect-eating birds also have certain likes and dislikes, and secure their animal food in a variety of places. Some forage on ground, others feed about trees and bushes, and still others glean a living from the atmosphere.

Very few birds eat potato beetles, but the rose-breasted grosbeak and bobwhite are fond of them. Others relish smooth caterpillars, but leave the hairy or spiny ones alone. But the cuckoos eat both and often so many of the spiny kind that the inner linings of their stomachs become pierced and coated with the spines and look as if lined with fur. The flicker specializes in the destruction of ants, more than fifty per cent of its food consisting of them. The bluebird and meadowlark are very fond of cutworms and grasshoppers, destroying thousands of them yearly.

The woodpecker, creeper, and nuthatch guard the trunks and branches of trees from the ravages of wood-boring beetles, grubs, and ants; the oriole, vireo, warbler, tanager, and chickadee protect their leaves and branches; the nighthawk, swift, swallow, and flycatcher glean pests from the atmosphere; and hosts of other birds are continually working in our interests, eating and destroying pests of all sorts. Every nook and corner is explored and guarded until it is a wonder that any of them escape. And where pests are numerous there also the birds as a rule are numerous, working in our interests and saving many a crop.

Finally, birds are worth attracting to one's premises in order that they may be studied more closely. They are among the most interesting and beautiful of creatures and have advantages over most other forms of animal and plant life for study purposes. When attracted to the yard by means of water, food, nesting devices, and trees, their colors, habits, songs, and flight may be observed to advantage. We may watch them as they court, feast, and play; how they build their nests, what materials they use, the size and color of their eggs; how, when, and what they feed their young; and we may also watch the antics of their young and how they learn to fly. And these lovely creatures will even come to your garden and yard, to your doors and windows, where you can enjoy all of these things. This alone makes it worth while for us to attract them and do our best to have them for close neighbors.

Female rose-breasted grosbeak enjoying a bath.

Chapter II

BIRDBATHS AND DRINKING FOUNTAINS

ONE of the simplest and most effective ways of attracting birds is to provide them with some kind of birdbath. Certain animals dislike water and stay away from it whenever possible, as, for example, the house cat, but birds do not seem to mind it in the least. Many of them seem extremely happy and contented when splashing around in a pan or pool of water, and at that they are ordinarily far from being dull and unhappy creatures. The moment many of them catch sight of a pool of water their feathers begin to fluff out as if in pleasant anticipation of the bath they intend to take.

Take a walk along a stream some warm summer day and you will see many happy groups of birds along its shores enjoying themselves. As a rule, you will find them in tiny pools or trickles along the shore. Here is a catbird all wet and bedraggled, flapping its wings and sending the water flying in all directions, there a song sparrow, a goldfinch, or a yellow warbler taking a dip, and yonder other species. Swallows love to circle and dip above streams, ponds, and marshes. Tree swallows sometimes are to be seen playing a game of follow the leader, one little bird dipping and lightly touching the surface of the water, then another, and another, and all of them, strangely enough, touch the water at exactly the same spot.

Not only do most songbirds seem to be strongly attracted by water and enjoy taking a drenching bath in it, but they actually need it and suffer from thirst if none is available. To be sure, birds ordinarily have little trouble securing enough water for drinking purposes. During periods of rainy weather there are pools everywhere, and there are ponds, marshes, and streams somewhere in most neighborhoods. Then, too, a few drops of dew are enough to satisfy them. Woodlands, yards, fields, and pastures, however, are farther from water, and when the weather is hot and dry, the birds are likely to suffer in such places.

An easy way of showing that birds are strongly attracted by water is to point out that many of them habitually live or frequent places near streams, ponds, and marshes. The best spots to go for bird study are the brushy and wooded shores of ponds and streams.

There you will find birds of a dozen or more species, flitting gaily about, feasting, singing, and nesting. And the best places to go when looking for the nests of many species during the breeding season are to meadows, pastures, and woods that are near ponds and ravines.

The birds are quite sure to visit your birdbath even though there are other watering places in the neighborhood. And many of them seem to enjoy taking a bath even when it is raining, as if the weather puts the idea into their little heads. But they are far from bashful at other times, and during hot, dry weather will visit a birdbath with great regularity, and it is at such times that one attracts them in the largest numbers and is of greatest service to them.

Not long ago, during the month of January, we watched a blue jay at one of our birdbaths. There was a little ice in the dish, and the bird tried its best to take a bath. It pecked at the ice, squatted, and fluttered its wings in a most comical way. It tried again and again, and when it left another flew to the dish and tried its best to secure a drink and take a bath.

No doubt the easiest and simplest way of providing the birds with a bath and drinking fountain is to set out a shallow pan filled with water. The pan may be placed on the ground near a bush, or set on a post, stump, or ledge, if there are any cats or other bird enemies in the neighborhood that are likely to pounce upon your guests. Birds often splash around in water until they are wet from head to foot and their feathers so soaked that they are unable to fly and

Kingbird near a pan birdbath.

fall easy victims to cats. If the pan is deep, rocks of various sizes should be placed in it, so the water will be shallow.

One of the easiest and simplest ways of making a birdbath is to make it out of concrete. A birdbath of this sort is not brightly colored, rather it has a dull, stonelike appearance and blends well with the greens, grays, and browns about it. Consequently, it has advantages over pans made of metal and enameled in various decorative ways. It also has a rough surface and the birds have less trouble perching on it.

The first thing to do when making anything out of concrete is to make a form into which to pour the mortar. The forms for cement work are usually made from lumber. But it is not a very practical material out of which to make a form for a concrete birdbath, unless you are a skilled workman or the shape very simple. A form for making a simple concrete birdbath is most easily prepared by digging a saucer-shaped hole in the ground about two feet in diameter and four inches deep. Naturally, the diameter may vary a good deal, as the size is a personal matter; you may want a larger or smaller one and consequently the form must be made accordingly.

When preparing the concrete, use four parts of coarse sand or gravel and one of cement. In other words, first take four shovelfuls of gravel and dump them into a box, and then add one of cement. Mix the gravel and cement thoroughly with a hoe until the mixture is of uniform color throughout. Then add a small quantity of water and mix thoroughly once more. Add water until you have a thick, flowing mortar. Then plaster the mortar about the bottom and sides of the hole until you have a layer about two inches in thickness, finishing the work by smoothing and patting the mortar to make the finished product hard, water-tight, and fairly smooth. Allow the concrete to dry a few days and your birdbath is ready for use.

Perhaps there are some who think that the making of things out of concrete is a complicated undertaking and entails much work. However, the making of a simple object out of concrete is very easy provided

there is no complicated form to make. A simple birdbath like the one just described is not much harder
to make than a mud pie; actually it is a pan made
out of mud, and any child can dig a hole in the
ground and use this for a form. You mix earth with
water when making mud, and from this you fashion
pies and other things with your hands. You mix
gravel, cement, and water when making anything
out of concrete, and secure a mixture that often is
called "mud" by masons and plasterers, and you
fashion the pan with your hands, a trowel, a large
spoon, or a thin piece of lumber whittled into shape.

If there are no bird enemies in the neighborhood,
this bath may be placed on the ground beneath a
tree or bush in a corner of the yard, otherwise it
should be placed on the top of a post, stump, ledge,
or in the crotch of a tree. A pedestal may be made
for it by cutting a small log four to six feet in length
from the trunk of a small tree, or large post. A rustic
standard proves well adapted to a concrete birdbath
of this kind. This may be made from the trunks of
small trees or suitable branches from larger ones.
Make or cut three of the branches the same length
and use them for uprights. Fasten these together
securely by means of crosspieces and bevel the tops
and bottoms so that the device stands firmly on the
ground and that the bath or basin rests securely on
the tops of all the uprights. A pedestal may be made
also by taking a piece about six feet long from the
trunk of a small crotched tree. The part taken should
include the crotch which should have at least three
branches. The crotch should be trimmed so that the

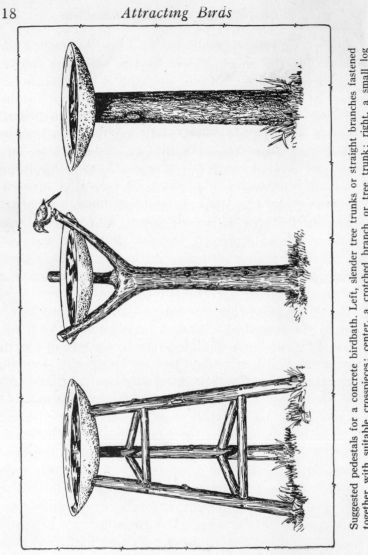

Suggested pedestals for a concrete birdbath. Left, slender tree trunks or straight branches fastened together with suitable crosspieces; center, a crotched branch or tree trunk; right, a small log four to six feet long.

basin will rest securely in it. The illustration on page 18 will give you an idea of how the three pedestals here mentioned are made.

Birdbaths of many kinds may be purchased from supply houses and dealers at a variety of prices. Fancy and elaborate ones may be made by people skillful in the use of tools, lumber, and concrete, but here we are not concerned with anything that is hard to make or which is expensive. This book is devoted to simple devices, most of them so simple that they may be made by a child at little or no cost.

Three bluebirds and a brown thrasher at our pan birdbath.

Chapter III

OUR BIRDBATHS

THE first birdbath we ever had was nothing more than a small pan fourteen inches in diameter and three inches deep, which was filled with water and placed on the ground beneath a bush near the kitchen window. We lived in a small city in the valley of the Red River of the North at the time. Our home was less than eighty rods from the banks of the stream, on a great prairie where only a few trees were to be seen. Most of the trees in this section grew along the shores of the river, about farm homes where they had been planted, and in yards of cities and villages.

Our city was thickly dotted with noble trees and consequently well suited to bird life.

There were many trees in our yard, and a row of small trees and bushes ran the length of the west side taking the place of a fence. The migrating birds followed the river on their northward journey, and one could take walks up and down its wooded shores and see birds of many species. Naturally, when the birds reached the city they made journeys farther inland, visiting yards a short distance from the stream as well as those along its shores. They visited our yard in large numbers and enabled us to observe and study many species from the house.

A pair of friendly robins built a nest in the crotch of a box elder in the front yard, where they reared a family of lively youngsters. The parent birds hunted earthworms in the yard and garden and eventually became very tame. I had a pile of pine wood which I was splitting and noticed that many of the sticks were honeycombed and harbored white grubs; these fell to the ground as the splitting proceeded and were discovered by the robins. The birds were on hand to get the grubs I dislodged whenever I split wood afterwards, discarding all other food in preference to them. They hopped about me until they discovered a grub; then they hurried toward me, secured it and carried it off and fed it to their young. Sometimes they took grubs from my shoes, on which I laid a few of the "bugs" to see what the birds would do about it.

A pair of Arkansas kingbirds had a nest near the top of a tall cottonwood just across the street. We saw them daily darting from their lofty perches after insects, or heard them as they chattered in their out-of-the-ordinary and noisy way. A chebec often perched on a telephone wire near the kitchen window, where it raised its little bill and said *"chee- beck"* over and over, singing its odd harsh monotonous song so continuously that we had little trouble identifying it and learning its name.

Naturally, since the birds found our trees and bushes attractive, and frequently visited us, they soon discovered the pan of water and had many good times about it, drinking and bathing to their hearts' content. The most interesting birds that visited our pan birdbath were the Harris sparrows. There were many of these birds in the neighborhood, and they visited us with great regularity. Harris sparrows are among our largest sparrows. In summer they have black faces, crowns, and throats and are easily identified, since they look quite unlike most other sparrows. Ovenbirds and warblers also visited our birdbath, together with others that I have long since forgotten.

Our next birdbath also was made from an old dishpan I set in a suitable hole dug in the ground. This pan had an eventful history, for when we shipped it to our present home it must have been in some kind of accident. It looked like a piece of crumpled tin or granite. I straightened it out as best I could and used it for a birdbath. I placed a number of rocks in it before I filled it with water, since it was too deep for a birdbath. Some of the rocks projected above the surface of the water and pro-

A gay party at one of our cement birdbaths. The two birds in
the foreground are bluebirds, the one near the left center looks
like a chippy, and at least one of the others is a young oriole.

vided the birds with perching places while they were
drinking, bathing, preening, and resting. Dozens of
species of birds soon found the old pan and the
water it held. It was hot and dry that summer, and
there was no other water to be had within a quarter
of a mile of us, which made our crude birdbath very
popular with the birds of the neighborhood.

Many bluebirds lived and nested in the neighborhood, and sometimes five or six, and again as many
as fifteen or eighteen of these pretty and useful birds

visited our birdbath. They wandered near and far after the nesting season, visiting the neighboring fields, pastures, and wooded hills, but often came our way for a drink of water and a bath. They usually were to be seen in family parties consisting of the father and mother birds and three, four, or five youngsters. The male could easily be distinguished from the others, because he had bright blue above and red on the breast; the mother was paler, and the young birds had short tails and spotted breasts. These family parties visited our birdbath many times a day, and, as a rule, all the birds bathed and secured a drink at the same time but were not quarrelsome. Sometimes, however, two or three families of these same birds were at the pan at one time, then there was a good deal of quarreling, since the members of one family tried their best to drive the others away.

A pair of Baltimore orioles had a nest somewhere in the neighborhood, no doubt in a large bur oak northeast of the house, since I afterwards found a pouched nest hanging to one of the outer branches. These birds began visiting our birdbath shortly after the young left the nest. We could hear them all day long, chirping as they hunted caterpillars and other bugs about the tops of the trees in the oak grove. Occasionally they stopped hunting food and fluttered to the ground near the bath, reminding one of a small shower of bright yellow leaves in autumn.

Sometimes the bluebirds and orioles arrived at the pan at about the same time; then, too, there was much quarreling, the bluebirds trying their best to drive off the orioles, and the orioles to chase the bluebirds. As a rule, the first birds to arrive stood their ground and refused to be driven off, and the late arrivals had to await their turn.

Brown thrashers are always interesting, and they are wonderful songsters. Their songs are loud, rich, and varied, and they always choose prominent perches when singing, such as the topmost twigs of trees and the tops of telephone poles. When otherwise engaged, they nearly always are to be found on or near the ground. When traveling short distances they go afoot or fly near the ground and make good use of trees and bushes to hide their movements. They usually nest in bushes and brush piles, but also build on the ground and the branches of trees if no other places are available, making the cradles of twigs and rootlets. There were many of these birds in the neighborhood, and they visited our birdbaths regularly. Only one thrasher secured a drink or enjoyed a bath at one time, since the first one there drove off any others that came along. Not until the bird at the bath was through did another get a chance to drink and bathe. And not only did they wage war upon one another but upon any other birds that happened to come near them.

A pair of rose-breasted grosbeaks also visited the pan from time to time, the male dressed in black and white and having a rose-colored breast, and the female looking like a large sparrow with a very stout bill. These birds, I am quite sure, did not nest near us, though I sometimes heard the male singing sweetly from the tops of the trees in the grove, or uttering his *"eek"* note.

The blue jays always proved of interest when at our birdbath. These birds are about as common and easy to attract by means of food and water as any birds to be found. They always are neat, clean, and attractive, and they have many interesting notes. *"Tee, tee, tee,"* they sometimes say in low conversational tones, as if passing along a choice bit of gossip they have heard, or are imparting a bit of valuable information; at other times they cry out *"here, here,"* much louder, as if trying to determine the whereabouts of some missing companion. One of their most common notes sounds like *"dee-jay, dee-jay,"* or *"jay, jay."* Sometimes they bob their heads and utter their queer *"gee-rul-lup, gee-rul-lup"*; this note also sounds a good deal like *"de-vel-op, de-vel-op."* Do blue jays know a thing or two about photographic films? I should like to know.

Not only did we find our blue-jay neighbors interesting and attractive but also well mannered and far from being as quarrelsome as many of the other birds that visited us. They usually came in small flocks, and the first ones at the bath called out *"here, here"* as if urging the others to hurry along. Perhaps they were trying to tell their companions that there was plenty of water in the birdbath and that there was no one around, not even another bird. I could just imagine them saying: *"Hurry, hurry! The water's fine. And there's not a person in sight. Hurry, hurry!"*

One of the queerest and most cautious of our guests was the flicker. He edged toward the pan very slowly indeed, often advancing a step or two and

One of the queerest and most cautious of our guests
was the flicker.

then hurrying off again twice as far perhaps. It took
him a long time to get to the pan, and when he did
get there, likely as not, he at once turned about and
hurried off again. Again he edged his way slowly
and cautiously to the pan, stopping every now and
then and looking carefully in every direction before
advancing. Eventually he reached the water a second
time, where he quickly made sure the coast was
clear, took a sip or two and a hasty bath, and then
at once departed.

Most of our bird neighbors became tame and confiding before the summer was far advanced. I secured
many pictures of them by setting the camera near
the pan and operating the shutter by means of a

long strong string. Some of our feathered neighbors
perched on the machine, pecked at its bright metal
parts, hopped or walked beneath it, and even perched
on the string fastened to the shutter.

And in what strange combinations our guests came.
Once a flicker and a red-headed woodpecker were
there at the same time, but both kept as far apart
as they could get without leaving entirely. One could
not help imagining they were just a little afraid or
suspicious of each other. At another time two orioles,
a red-headed woodpecker, and a kingbird were there,
once a robin and an oriole, and again a bluebird, a
brown thrasher, and an oriole.

That same summer I made two cement birdbaths
to take the place of the old dishpan. These were
about sixteen inches in diameter and two or three
inches deep in their deepest parts. These proved even
more popular than the old dishpan. I once counted
twenty-five birds about them at the same time.

Our birdbaths proved very popular with the birds
during the morning and evening hours and on rainy
days. The fact that it was raining, had just stopped
raining, or was about to rain caused the birds to
flock to them in large numbers. Birds are not as
active in the middle of the day as during the morning
and evening hours, and this, I suspect, caused our
little bathing beaches to be more or less deserted
when the sun was high.

So many birds visited our birdbaths, and they
came so often, that I decided to find out how many
visited them in a day. I kept a record of their number for a period of five hours, and from my count

estimated that seventy-five visited us each day for a bath and two hundred and twenty-five for a drink of water. At that rate, if my estimate was correct, we had eighteen thousand bird visitors during the months of June, July, August that year. This does not mean, however, that eighteen thousand different individuals visited us, since many of the birds visited us not once but perhaps a dozen times each day. One bird may have visited us several hundred times during the summer. I doubt if there were more than a hundred different individuals that made use of our birdbaths, but those one hundred individuals visited them nearly twenty thousand times during the summer. I also estimated that these birds took six thousand baths during the three months.

Our birdbaths proved themselves very effective magnets for attracting birds, drawing many species from all parts of the neighborhood to our yard, where they destroyed insects and weed seeds; and how much we learned from them, and how much pleasure they afforded us.

Twenty-five species of birds visited our birdbaths and secured places on our list during the summer. They are as follows:

Baltimore oriole	Meadowlark
Bluebird	Myrtle warbler
Blue jay	Orchard oriole
Brown thrasher	Palm warbler
Catbird	Phoebe
Cedar waxwing	Purple finch
Chipping sparrow	Red-headed woodpecker
Cowbird	Robin

Field sparrow
Flicker
Grackle
Junco
Kingbird

Rose-breasted grosbeak
Scarlet tanager
Vesper sparrow
White-throated sparrow

The white-breasted nuthatch always looks from side to side when feeding so as not to be surprised by some enemy.

Chapter IV

ATTRACTING BIRDS WITH FOOD

THE birds never go hungry in summer, because foods of all kinds are to be found everywhere and usually in such large quantities that they have more than enough. They become more or less hard to please, eating only that which pleases their palates and leaving the rest like overfed children. But in winter and during late spring snowstorms quite the opposite is true. The birds to be seen in December, January, and February are commonly known as winter birds, and include such species as the blue jay, white-breasted nuthatch, chickadee, slate-col-

31

ored junco, English sparrow, tree sparrow, downy, hairy, and red-headed woodpeckers, and many others. These birds are to be found where food is more or less abundant. Cardinals are attracted by wild berries and weed seeds; downy and hairy woodpeckers are found in deep woods; the red-headed woodpecker where acorns are plentiful; and juncos and tree sparrows where weed seeds are to be had.

How birds are governed in the choice of their winter haunts by a food supply is well illustrated by the red-headed woodpecker. This bird is to be seen in numbers where there are oak trees, since they furnish it with holes for nesting purposes and much of its winter food supply. In summer it lives largely upon insects, but during the cold weather it eats many acorns. This bird will live in a given place the year around if acorns are plentiful, but when they are scarce it winters far from its summer haunts. The red-headed woodpecker stores many acorns in autumn when they are to be had, hiding them beneath the loose bark of dead trees, in cracks and crevices, and in holes in the decayed wood of old stumps. If no suitable holes and cracks are to be found in partly decayed posts, stumps, and stubs, it makes some and neatly tucks an acorn into each.

The best way to attract birds in summer is to provide them with a birdbath, since they then need water for drinking purposes, and many of them enjoy taking a bath. But in winter providing them with food is the most effective way of inducing them to pay you a visit and live near you. Many of them will be your guests daily if they know food is to be had in your yard.

It is a good plan to make or set out your food tray, shelf, or other device in the fall, and to begin placing food on it long before the birds actually are in need of food and likely to make use of it. Occasionally, a bird visits it and learns to know its location; then when food becomes scarce and the snow deep, it knows where to find it.

Our winter birds may roughly be divided into two general classes by their food requirements. Some of them habitually live on bugs, grubs, beetles, caterpillars, grasshoppers, ants, plant lice, and so on, while others live largely on weed seeds, waste grain, and the like. Good examples of the former are the nuthatch, downy and hairy woodpeckers, and the chickadee, and of the latter the slate-colored junco and the tree sparrow. Some birds also eat both animal and vegetable foods. The best food perhaps, also the cheapest, you can secure for the insect eaters is beef suet. A large piece of this may be purchased for a few cents at any meat market, enough to last a number of birds a long time. And the cheapest, best, and easiest food to secure for the latter is oatmeal. If you offer the birds all they want of these simple foods, you can keep many of them happy and contented, yes, healthy and energetic, too, all winter long.

To be sure, many other foods may be offered the birds in winter: bread crumbs, meat scraps, seeds of various kinds, and ground and cracked grain, in fact most anything you have at hand for which you have no other use. Most foods, whether these be some we have on hand for ourselves, our livestock, or our poultry, may be offered the birds, so all of us can do something toward helping them in winter. Nevertheless, if you purchase anything, let it be rolled oats and beef suet. Both are very nourishing, cost but little, and may be purchased anywhere. From this I would have you understand that the matter of feeding and attracting winter birds is so easy and simple that a child can do it. To attract and help them you do not need to go to a great deal of trouble and expense.

A serviceable food tray for the birds may be quickly and easily made. All the materials you will need in order to make an excellent food tray are a board about a foot square, four short pieces of lath, and a little stick a foot or ten inches in length. Naturally, if you wish, you may purchase many fancy and high-priced foods and you may make or purchase elaborate feeding devices, but only two simple foods and a simple food tray are all that is required. And I

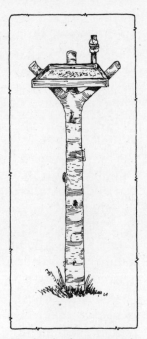

Simple food tray made from a piece of board a foot square, four short pieces of lath, and a small stick ten inches long. Standard made from small crotched tree trunk or branch.

actually believe that from the standpoint of the birds the simpler foods are the best. "Have horse sense and eat oatmeal" is an excellent and often necessary health slogan for children but not for the birds. The birds seem to realize that oatmeal makes good food. and one does not need to urge or encourage them to eat it by means of slogans. Use laths in making a rim for your tray in order to keep the food from blowing away. Fasten a stick at one corner to which suet may be tied. Place the tray on the top of a post. a ledge, or the branch of a tree, preferably south of the house, so that the building will protect your guests from cold north and west winds.

Many feeding devices are equipped with roofs and north walls, to keep out the snow and wind. This really is unnecessary, since a roof, if one is provided, does not keep out a great deal of snow anyway, and a building makes a much better windbreak than a wall on your tray. Even though your tray has a roof, it will be necessary to keep it free from snow and to supply it with food daily or whenever necessary.

The important point to remember is that the type of feeding device makes little difference to the birds but a constant supply of food does. The oatmeal may be spread on the tray, while the suet should be tied to the suet stick. Take a piece of suet the size of a walnut or small apple and tie it securely to the stick. Use several pieces of string and wind each in turn around and around the suet until it is held in place by a network. This will keep large birds from carrying off the whole piece, thus keeping you busy early and late putting out more. Force the birds to eat

This hairy woodpecker was an economical fellow. If a tiny p'ece of suet fell to the tray he picked it up and ate it before loosening another piece.

the suet in small quantities at the tray. Another good way to serve the suet is to grind or cut it into small pieces and then to place it on the tray with the oatmeal. If the suet is shaved from the large piece and the shavings in turn crumbled with the hand, a knife, or a small, thin piece of wood, it will be in small enough pieces to keep your guests from carrying it off in large pieces. The suet also may be inclosed in a wire mesh, a wire soap shaker, or some other similar device.

Other simple ways of feeding the birds in winter

are to tie suet, bread crusts, stale bread, popcorn, peanuts, and other foods to discarded Christmas trees, or to trample down the snow on the ground and spread oatmeal, finely ground suet, and other foods on it.

One of our most valuable birds, the bobwhite, is a winter bird, staying or living in a given region winter and summer alike. This chubby bird is timid and often needs help in winter, and to help it is often a hard problem. It will not come to a food tray like the woodpeckers, nuthatch, junco, chickadee, blue jay, and some of the other birds. Consequently, the person who wishes to help it must adopt other methods. While bobwhites seldom come to the house, they often visit the barnyard, hay and straw stacks, shocks of corn fodder, and other similar places. If grains and other foods are spread on the ground or snow near hay stacks, corn shocks, and trees, these birds are likely to find and eat them. Bobwhites also often travel from the base of one tree to the base of another, where they pick up nut meats and other foods wasted by the squirrels and woodpeckers, and, of course, will also eat grain if they find any. Likewise they often travel from one corn shock to another, and if one is hollowed out and food placed beneath it the birds are likely to visit, secure a hearty and welcome meal, and return to it again and again. Or a number of leafy branches may be secured, set on end, and their tops tied together so they form a tepee; beneath and about this food may be spread for these little wild chickens.

To help spring birds during belated snowstorms,

tie pieces of suet to posts, branches, and sticks. Your food tray should be kept well supplied with oatmeal and other foods. Remove the snow from a small piece of ground in the yard. Most of our first spring migrants feed largely from the ground and are sure to visit any bare patches to be found in the neighborhood, where they find seeds, earthworms, and insects. Consequently, they will be sure to find and feed from any spot from which the snow has been shovelled. Juncos, goldfinches, cardinals, sparrows of several species, and many other birds are likely to visit it for weed seeds and any stray insects they may find; and woodpeckers, chickadees, bluebirds, and robins will visit it for earthworms, cutworms, and other tidbits. Naturally, the spot may and should be made doubly useful by spreading other foods about it, such as oatmeal, bread crumbs, crumbled suet, meat scraps, seeds, and grains. Many storms are accompanied by strong winds that sweep the snow from exposed spots and pile it in drifts elsewhere. As soon as the storms are over, the birds visit the exposed and bare spots in search of food. To help them, spread food, most anything you have at hand for which you have no other use, on these bare spots, and many birds will enjoy a hearty meal.

A slate-colored junco enjoying a meal at the food tray on a very cold day in winter.

Chapter V

OUR FOOD TRAYS

WE had a few winter birds for neighbors even before we began to feed them in a systematic way. We live on a small farm containing twenty acres of ground, on which the birds were able to find something to eat even when we did not go to the trouble of making a tray and supplying it with suet and oatmeal. When acorns were plentiful, the red-headed woodpecker remained with us all winter long. Sometimes the red-bellied woodpecker paid us a visit. The blue jays and English sparrows also were in evidence, gleaning many a meal from refuse and waste grain to be found about the barn and henhouse. Bobwhites came to the barnyard and ran around the hay, straw, and fodder stacks, the trees, and buildings, and made sure that the jays and sparrows did not overlook anything. Naturally, too, since we had many oak trees, downy and hairy woodpeckers, nuthatches, chickadees, and brown creepers visited them from time to time, hunting insects and other pests on their trunks and branches.

One winter a slate-colored junco lived near us, roosting, I am quite sure, in the woodpile and gleaning crumbs and other tidbits from the sweepings. Each day this hardy little bird was to be seen, and he found enough food to keep him happy and energetic. Although slate-colored juncos are generally to be seen in flocks during the autumn, winter, and spring, living on weed seeds to be found in fields, waste places, and open pastures, one or two of them are often to be found living far from others of their kind. The first junco I ever saw was one that daily visited the yard of a rural school where I was teaching. He feasted on bread crumbs and other food he found about the doorstep.

The first thing I did when I decided to try to attract birds to the yard, by means of food in winter, was to trample down the snow on a spot below a south window and spread oatmeal and crumbs on it. Juncos, tree sparrows, and English sparrows found this shortly after I had the food in place and came in groups to feed there. Juncos are also known as slate-colored snowbirds. They are slate-colored above, white underneath, and have white outer tail feathers and straw-colored bills. They are small birds, being about as large as English sparrows. It was great fun to watch them eating oatmeal, since they worked their bills very rapidly when eating, as if carefully chewing each bite of food before swallowing it. They often uttered their low, contented *"chew, chew, chew"* notes when feasting, and chew is exactly what they all did. At other times they uttered notes of alarm or anger, sharp, clicking notes, lower, but otherwise much like the clicking alarm note of the brown thrasher. When it was very cold they came all fluffed out, and they squatted on the snow, covering their feet with their soft warm feathers. They seemed to know how to keep their feet warm when the thermometer registered twenty degrees below zero. On cold days, too, they always seemed sluggish and not as alert as at other times, as if all their energy were needed to keep them warm; but on warmer days they stood up, hopped briskly about, and flitted playfully here and there.

Tree sparrows are dressed in gray and brown, being typical of their group, but have reddish crowns, light wing bars, and round dark spots on their breasts by means of which they are recognized. They are about as large as juncos, and live in flocks. Usually mixed groups of tree sparrows, juncos, and perhaps a few English sparrows haunt roadsides, fence rows, old fields, waste places, the borders of streams, and railway right-of-ways.

I next secured a large piece of beef suet at the meat market and tied small pieces of it to a number of trees and posts either in or near the yard. I fas-

Blue jays feeding on suet and other foods placed on a stub for them. Jays are always wide-awake and alert and quick to discover threatening danger — "Safety First" is their motto.

tened a larger piece securely to an old oak stub five feet from an east window. The blue jays found the suet on the stub within a day or two, but only after discovering and feasting on some pieces fastened to trees south of the house, and to the posts east of the yard. After that I fed them entirely from the stub. I spread some crumbs and oatmeal on the flat top and this attracted several English sparrows. I was quite sure that since the jays and sparrows had found my feeding station that other birds also would soon find it. Nor was I mistaken. Birds seem to know very well what other birds in the neighborhood are doing and finding to eat, learning it as quickly and surely as though they published and read newspapers. Not long after the jays began feeding from the stub, a nuthatch made his appearance. He worked his way about until he found the suet, then proceeded to have a hearty meal. Eventually, he dislodged a piece as large as a pea; this he at once carried off and hid in a crack or crevice somewhere near by for future use.

The nuthatch is a chubby little bird six inches in length with a gray back, black crown and nape, short square tail brightened with white. He has pure-white cheeks, throat, breast, and underparts. His white breast or vest has given him the name white-breasted nuthatch and distinguishes him from a smaller nuthatch with reddish underparts, the red-breasted nuthatch. The female has a gray crown. The most common note of this bird is a queer grunting *"ank, ank,"* or *"yank, yank,"* which it often utters with its bill closed. The throat pulsates with each note, although the mandibles may not move at all. Sometimes, when near another nuthatch, or other bird, it seems to talk to it in low *"twits." "Twit, twit — How do you do; twit, twit — I am surprised to see you here; twit, twit — this suet is delicious, isn't it?"* And it sings an odd but pleasant *"kwee, kwee — kwee, kwee"* song on the mornings early in spring. It is a topsy-turvy bird, going head first down the trunks and branches of trees and hanging to the lower side of a branch as easily as a fly clings to the ceiling. It likes to have a food tray or piece of suet to itself, driving off its mate as well as other birds, unless the latter are large and aggressive fellows, such as the blue jay.

Shortly after this I nailed a board four inches wide and five feet in length to the top of the stub, in such a way that it extended toward the nearest window, the inner end being but two feet from it. To the end of this I fastened a simple food tray, like that described in the preceding chapter, placed some crumbs and oatmeal on it, and tied a piece of suet to the stick fastened to one corner. After that I placed no more food on the stub, forcing the birds to come to the tray for it. Since the birds were used to feeding from the stub, they soon fed from the tray without fear.

The next birds to find my feeding device were the downy and hairy woodpeckers. Downy made his way to the tray and suet stick with but little fussing, because he noticed that the nuthatch visited them. Occasionally he uttered a *"peek"* note of alarm to bolster up his courage, but eventually he did so without making a sound. He often came and left without our knowing the fact. He often sat for a time when feeding as if deep in thought. He hammered but little at the suet, but frequently sat with his bill down and picked up tiny pieces of suet with his tongue. The hairy woodpecker, on the other hand, always uttered sharp notes of alarm when on or near the tray. He generally spent some time about the bur oak near the corner of the house before going to it; up this tree he hopped, secured a bug now and then, looked carefully in every direction to make sure no enemies were near, and uttered sharp *"peek"* notes. When he reached the tray, he hammered vigorously at the suet, ate a hearty meal, and then flew off again. The downy and hairy woodpeckers are both dressed in black and white; the males have red patches on the backs of their heads; and they look so much alike that they are likely to be confused, unless you remember that the hairy is the larger of the two. The hairy is nearly as large as the robin, whereas the downy is about the size of the English sparrow.

The next bird to find our tray and suet stick, and our suet and rolled oats, was a bird we were hoping would come, the cheerful little chickadee. How happy we were when we heard him announce his arrival one cold winter day with a merry *"chick-a-dee-dee!"*

The next bird to find our tray and suet stick was a bird we were hoping would come, the cheerful little chickadee.

And not only was there one chickadee but several of them. They ate suet mainly, but also helped themselves to the oatmeal. And how tame they were! We often stood at the window and watched them. They looked our way from time to time, their bright black eyes twinkling merrily, greeted us with a *"chick-a-dee-dee,"* or *"dee-dee,"* then resumed their feasting.

These birds are tiny fellows about five inches in length. They are grayish in color, but have black crowns or caps, black bibs or bow neckties, and long tails. They are among our most cheerful and happy birds, staying with us all winter long. They live mainly on small insects, their larvae and eggs, which they glean from trees, where they hang and swing, bob and flit, both in winter and summer alike. Their bright eyes are ever on the lookout for tiny pests and their sharp bills ever ready to dislodge and destroy them. They often are to be heard whistling a sweet song, a clear ringing *"fee-bee, fee-bee,"* which reminds one of the song of the phoebe. One of the chickadees that visited our food tray had a sore foot and always hopped about on but one. These little sprites have their troubles, too, though they always seem happy and contented.

A red-headed and a red-bellied woodpecker also visited our tray. The red-headed woodpecker came just a few times, only then because he was curious as to what it was all about, and not because he was hungry. This bird is so thrifty and stores so many acorns that he never goes hungry, but often the jays and squirrels find it to their advantage to make raids on his many storehouses. Then the woodpeckers scold and sputter and utter sharp *"kit-ti, kit-ti"* notes, dash this way and that, bob their heads, and make things decidedly lively. This bird is ten inches in length, or about as large as the robin, has a black-and-white body, wings, and tail, and a bright-red head, neck, and throat. Wide white bars run across its black wings.

The red-bellied woodpecker has finely barred black-and-white plumage, is about ten inches long, has a red forehead, crown, and nape, and reddish underparts. The female has a gray crown. It resembles the red-headed woodpecker in its habits, living principally on insects and nuts, and being irregularly migratory, sometimes even spending the winter north of its summer home, since it does not mind snow and cold weather if it is able to find enough to eat. It has a harsh call note, which sounds to me like *"cha, cha, cha,"* which it often utters in a long rolling series. The red-headed woodpecker, aside from its *"kit-ti, kit-ti"* notes, has some others also, the most common being a loud *"charr-charr-rr-rr-r"* which is heard during the mating and nesting season mainly. Then, too, it often beats a lively *"rat-a-tat-tat"* on a piece of sheet iron or the dry, resonant branch of a tree.

The old oak stub I first used as a standard for my bird food tray, I cut and used for fuel, and since have had to replace it with several others. One year I cut and set a crotched maple branch near an east window, and to this fastened the tray, but the next winter I made a standard for it out of the trunk of a young crotched box elder. It is easy to provide a food tray with a standard, since a small post, a crotched branch, or the trunk of a tree will do. If the post or branch is driven into the ground before it freezes up, it will be so firmly set by the time the birds begin coming to your tray that the strongest wind cannot upset it. In midwinter the post or branch may be set in the snow, by pouring water around it and allowing it to freeze. The ice or frozen snow will hold the post or branch firmly in place.

I have always placed our tray near a window, so that we could watch and study our bird guests to the best advantage. Then, too, I have been able to secure pictures of many of them easily. I made a wooden frame with a circular hole for the lower half of the window nearest the tray. When I wish to take pictures of our feathered guests, I raise the lower sash, insert the wooden frame, set up the camera, and then wait for the birds to arrive. The frame gives me something to hide behind and it shuts out the cold. I am able to stand behind it, watching the birds without being seen, and photograph them without alarming or frightening them off.

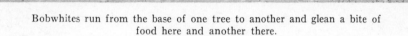

Bobwhites run from the base of one tree to another and glean a bite of food here and another there.

Chapter VI

OTHER WINTER-BIRD NEIGHBORS

THE brown creeper often pays us a visit in winter, though it never has ventured to our food tray and suet stick. Still, there are at least two good reasons why it comes. In the first place, we have many trees in and near the yard, and about these it can hunt all sorts of insects. Then, too, it, no doubt, finds many small pieces of suet that have been hidden about the trunks and branches of the trees by the thrifty nuthatch. The brown creeper, which is about five and one-half inches in length and of slender build, is practically always to be seen on the trunks of trees. It always travels up trees, carefully searching for insects hidden in the bark, not stopping until it gets near the top; then it drops to the base of another and travels up this in turn. It differs from the nuthatch in that it travels up trees, not down them. It is brownish in color, has a long, sharp bill, and a long tail with stiff pointed feathers. The stiff pointed tail quills serve as braces and are of help to it in climbing trees. If you listen carefully, when near one, you are likely to hear its shrill *"tseep";* but this is uttered in such a weak voice that you can hardly hear it.

Some of our prettiest and most welcome bird neighbors have never visited our food tray, but they came to the yard for another good reason. They are the cardinals, or cardinal grosbeaks, birds about nine inches in length with prominent crests and long tails. They resemble sparrows in many ways, and they are hardy and stay with us all winter long. Many people think that they migrate in autumn and winter far to the south, but this is not true. Each year I read news items in the daily paper to the effect that someone has seen a cardinal and that the seeing of the bird is a sign of spring. However, the seeing of a cardinal, which may be seen in December, January, and February as well as in June, July, and August, is not a sign of spring, rather it is a sign that this bird is hardy and lives in a given region, winter and summer alike.

We have many birds that are red in color, such as the scarlet tanager, painted bunting, vermilion flycatcher, and cardinal, and many also which are prominently marked with red. However, few if any of them are exactly the same shade of color. The shade of red found on the plumage of the scarlet tanager is quite different from that of the vermilion flycatcher, or the lovely rose-red found on the breast and underneath the wings of the male rose-breasted grosbeak, or that on the breast of the bluebird. Robin red-breast has his suit brightened with red; the same is true of the red-winged blackbird, the red-start, ruby-throated hummingbird, and others. The male cardinal grosbeak is cardinal-red in color, although he has some black about the head, while the female is grayish above and has a reddish crest, wings, and tail, and a reddish wash underneath. Naturally she is almost as attractive as her lord.

But why do the cardinals visit us in winter? They come to feed on the berries of our Virginia creepers and the wild grapes, and to glean seeds from the tall weeds to be found in the near-by fields and waste places. Last winter seven or eight of them at a time visited our vines for the frozen berries to be found on them. These birds utter a musical *"cheep"* from time to time, and when we hear this note we know that some of them are near the house.

Just west of our place there is a large field overgrown with weeds, where tree sparrows, juncos, goldfinches, and English sparrows are to be seen all winter long. Whenever I see groups of juncos and sparrows feeding there, I always look closely to see if there are any cardinals with them. One morning I frightened eight cardinals from a depression where the weeds were tall and thick. The pretty red birds flew across the street and settled in some young oaks, where I was able to observe them.

A few days later a large flock of sparrows was feeding in the field, and with them were the cardinals. This flock of cardinals has visited us many times, coming to the vine for berries, feeding on weed seeds in the garden, and perching in trees about the house. Cardinals resemble sparrows in having stout beaks, long tails, and much the same call or alarm note. They also live largely upon vegetable matter, such as seeds and berries. In the spring they are frequently to be heard singing a song so loud and unusual as not to be easily forgotten. And the birds have more than one whistled song. Sometimes they seem to say *"whit, whit, whit, whit, whit,"* at other times *"whit, whip, whip-whee-u, whip-whee-u, whip-whee-u, whit,"* and again something else.

Though fox sparrows are not winter birds, we helped a number of them one spring during a severe snowstorm. There were many of them, and they spent much of their time in a thicket west of the house, associating with some juncos which they resemble in their habits. Juncos and fox sparrows are fond of thickets, and both feed largely on the ground, where they scratch in the dirt and among the leaves, with both feet at once, however, not one at a time like a hen. The fox sparrows were very musical that spring, singing most freely in the morning, their song being loud and clear, more like that of the lark sparrow than those of chipping, field, tree, vesper, or song sparrows. To help the birds, I cleaned the snow from a piece of ground near the barn and another east of the house. Many fox sparrows found and fed from the bare ground near the barn, scratching in the moist black earth and securing many earthworms and other tidbits which they ate with relish. We spread some cracked grain, ground feed, oatmeal, crumbs, and crumbled boiled egg on the bare spot near the house, and here seven species of birds came for food: robins, bluebirds, blue jays, vesper sparrows, English sparrows, juncos, and a hairy woodpecker. The fox sparrows remained with us for many days and gave me the best opportunity I have ever had for enjoying their wonderful songs. These birds are reddish-brown in color above, have streaked breasts and sides, and a blotch of brown in the middle of the breast. They are about as large as the bluebird, and, because of their brownish plumage and streaked breasts, resemble thrushes, and often they are mistaken for them.

Bobwhites are rather common in our vicinity. In winter they live in flocks and wander from place to place in search of food. Any walk across the drifted fields and pastures is sure to result in seeing some of them, or the finding of their tracks in the snow. We often see bevies of them from the house, the chubby birds running or walking across the fields, from one patch of weeds or grass to another, or from one shock of corn to the next. They often cuddle down on the sunny side of a corn shock, tree, building, or other object and remain there for a time, resting and enjoying the sunshine. Sometimes large flocks visit the yard, the birds walking about the house, making their way from bush to bush, but eventually going to the barnyard, always traveling single file.

One cold winter day we looked out through an east window and saw a large flock of bobwhites sitting quietly beneath a small box elder only a few feet away. Our corn shocks, stacks of hay and straw, buildings, and trees attract these birds, especially since most of them stand on the south slope of a broad, low hill. The birds come to us for waste grain and grass seed, for shelter from the cold north and west winds, and for a rest and a sun bath.

But they also come for another reason. As previously stated, we generally have many red-headed woodpeckers for winter neighbors, these thrifty, independent fellows staying in the neighborhood when acorns are plentiful but wintering elsewhere when they are scarce. Red-headed woodpeckers are our most thrifty birds, storing acorns all autumn long for the cold, stormy winter ahead, and making use of holes, cracks, crevices, and other suitable places in every stump, post, and tree in the vicinity. And all winter long they visit their numerous storehouses and feast on the nuts. When feeding, they waste some of the food, littering the snow beneath them with shells and bits of acorn kernels. We also have many gray

Storehouse of the red-headed woodpecker.

squirrels for neighbors, and they, too, eat many acorn and waste parts of them. The bobwhites are well aware of the feeding habits of the red-headed woodpeckers and gray squirrels, and visit all the oak trees in the neighborhood from time to time, walking, running, or flying from the base of one tree to the base of another and gleaning a bite of food here and another there.

Although the tree sparrows sometimes come to our feeding station for oatmeal, they come much less often than the juncos or snowbirds. Nevertheless, we see much of them, for they visit our thickets and fields with great regularity for seeds of various kinds.

Last winter a large flock of snow buntings visited us for several days, feeding east of the house in the garden, where many tall weeds projected from the snow. The birds often took to their wings and circled and wheeled about for a time before settling on the snow, or the weeds, before resuming their feeding. Some of them clung to the tops of the weeds, where they pecked at and ate the seeds, dislodging many which fell to the snow. Other birds sat or ran around in the snow and picked up and ate the seeds which had fallen.

One winter we lived in a city of a half million inhabitants, where we had a large yard in which there were a number of ash trees. That winter a large flock of purple finches visited us regularly for the paddle-shaped seeds. Purple finches are about six inches long, the males being rose-red or pinkish-red in color and the females gray and brown and more or less streaked.

Near us also grew several mountain ash trees which bore many bunches of red berries, and these attracted flocks of cedar waxwings to the neighborhood. Cedar waxwings are about the size of the bluebird and have soft grayish-brown plumage, prominent crests, black markings about the head, and yellow bars across the ends of their tails. They are nomadic in their habits, being here one day and gone the next, wandering all about the countryside and living mainly on wild berries. They are sociable birds living in flocks much of the year. They have soft lisping *"tseep"* notes which you are quite sure to hear when there is a flock about, and they are expert flycatchers, often darting from their perches and catching insects on the wing.

The Bohemian waxwings resemble the cedar waxwings to a great extent but are seen much less often. They spend most of their time north of the United States and visit us only occasionally in winter. The Bohemian waxwings also are larger than cedar waxwings, they have darker plumage, and their notes are louder and have more of a ringing quality. Like cedar waxwings they have plum-colored tints about the plumage of their heads, necks, and foreparts of the body, black markings about the head, and yellow bars across the ends of their tails, but differ in having white and yellow patches on the wings. Though I see cedar waxwings many times in the course of a year, I have seen Bohemian waxwings but once, that being last year, when a large flock paid us a visit and stayed with us for three or four days. Something attracted the birds to the neighborhood, and this I soon learned to be the red berries of our asparagus. The birds stayed in the neighborhood until they had stripped our asparagus plants, then moved on to some other patch perhaps, but eventually returned to their real home far to the north.

Most of my winter bird neighbors are peaceful and useful, but sometimes I have others that are just the reverse. During severe winters I often see a goshawk in the neighborhood, either perching quietly in some distant tree or flying by in search of prey. This large hawk is a blue darter and very destructive, killing and eating bobwhites, squirrels, and other birds and animals. It comes to this neighborhood, I am quite sure, to prey upon the squirrels and bobwhites. Two years ago one caught and killed a bobwhite a short distance west of the house. Luckily, it is a rare bird, living for the most part north of the United States and visiting us only occasionally in winter.

Sometimes, too, at night, we hear "hoot owls" (great horned and barred owls) near the house. These nocturnal visitors, no doubt, are hunting birds, flying squirrels, rats, and mice in the neighborhood. And sometimes we see a sharp-shinned hawk. I once shot and killed one of these hawks just after it had made a meal of a slate-colored junco it had caught near the barn. I thought at first it might be a Cooper hawk, judging by its apparent size, but was surprised, when I picked it up, to find that it was no larger than a blue jay and of slender build. The long tail, which is square at the outer corners, makes up about half the total length of twelve inches. Its slender body, long tail, and short wings enable it to fly with great speed and to overtake and catch smaller birds while they are in full flight, something many hawks cannot do.

Wren box made from a tin can and two pieces of wood.

Tin is not advisable; too Becomes hot in summer!

Chapter VII

NESTING BOXES AND SHELVES

SOME birds may be attracted to the yard by means of nesting boxes and others by shelves. The birds likely to make use of boxes are those which habitually nest in hollow trees, branches, posts, and stumps — the woodpeckers, house wren, bluebird, purple martin, white-breasted nuthatch, chickadee, and tree swallow. Those likely to make use of shelves are birds which naturally build in more open locations, on the branches of trees, ledges, and about the eaves and rafters of buildings. Good examples of such birds are the robin, phoebe, and barn swallow.

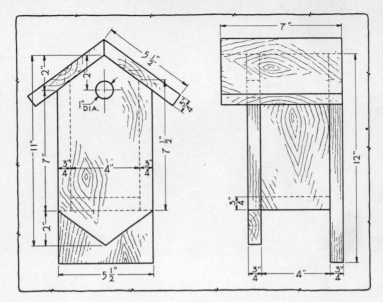

A simple wren box.

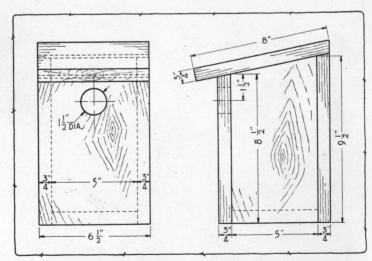

This bluebird house is simple and sturdy and may be covered with bark as shown in the illustration on page 71.

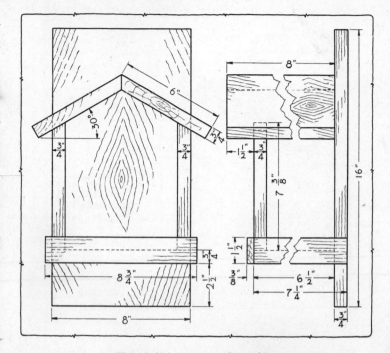

This shelf is open on three sides.

Many of these birds are easily attracted by means of boxes and shelves because they need them for nesting and protection. Formerly these birds were able to find enough dead and hollow trees and stubs to furnish them with nesting places. But now there is a scarcity of suitable places in many neighborhoods. Men have cut our forests, cleared away all the underbrush, and drained swamps, to make room for fields, railways, bridges, roads, towns, villages, and cities, thus robbing the birds of nesting places. And since

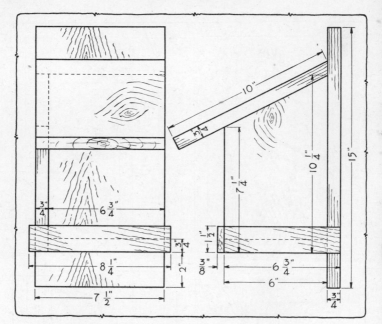

This shelf may be left open on two or three sides.

we have robbed the birds of their natural nesting sites we should try to replace them with others.

Since we build our homes and other buildings largely from lumber, most of us at once choose this material when making bird boxes and houses. And many neat and serviceable nesting boxes may be made from lumber. The first question likely to arise in connection with the use of lumber is this: Shall I use old or new lumber? The lumber used should look as much as possible like the wood or bark of trees, stubs, posts, and stumps, and this is old weather-beaten lumber. Many birds are afraid of

Robin shelf.

new, freshly painted and gaudy boxes. However, new lumber may be used for making bird boxes, but it should be painted a dull gray, brown, or green, the colors Mother Nature uses on trees, stubs, and posts. Copy nature as nearly as possible when painting your bird box and you will be more successful than if you use bright colors human beings are likely to think more attractive. Nevertheless, old weather-beaten boards are better than new ones that have been painted, because they already resemble the color of trees and stubs.

Birds that are likely to make use of nesting boxes

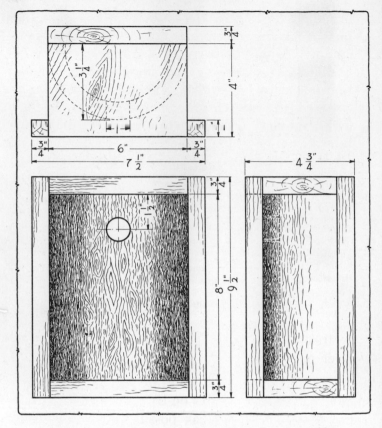

Dimensions for wren box shown in illustration on page 70.

have certain likes and dislikes, and these one should know and cater to in order to build houses to their liking. Naturally, too, the size of the box and entrance hole should be adapted to the bird, flickers needing much larger boxes than house wrens and wood ducks larger ones than bluebirds. Some birds

like their boxes near the ground, others want them
farther up, and some prefer houses with many rooms,
notably the purple martin.

About the easiest way of giving you the information in regard to the likes and dislikes of birds, the
size of boxes and entrance holes, and the height at
which the houses should be placed is by means of a
table. The following table* gives this information
for thirteen common birds — birds that often nest in
boxes that are set out for them:

Name	Floor	Depth	Entrance	Height
Bluebird	5 x 5 in.	8 in.	1½ in.	5 to 10 ft.
Chickadee	4 x 4 in.	8 in.	1⅛ in.	6 to 15 ft.
Tufted titmouse	4 x 4 in.	8 to 10 in.	1¼ in.	6 to 15 ft.
White-breasted nuthatch	4 x 4 in.	8 to 10 in.	1¼ in.	12 to 20 ft.
House wren	4 x 4 in.	6 to 8 in.	⅞ in.	6 to 10 ft.
Tree swallow	5 x 5 in.	6 in.	1½ in.	10 to 15 ft.
Crested flycatcher	6 x 6 in.	8 to 10 in.	2 in.	8 to 20 ft.
Flicker	7 x 7 in.	16 to 18 in.	2½ in.	8 to 20 ft.
Red-headed woodpecker	6 x 6 in.	12 to 15 in.	2 in.	12 to 20 ft.
Hairy woodpecker	6 x 6 in.	12 to 15 in.	2 in.	12 to 20 ft.
Downy woodpecker	4 x 4 in.	8 to 10 in.	1¼ in.	6 to 20 ft.
Screech owl	8 x 8 in.	12 to 15 in.	3 in.	10 to 30 ft.
Sparrow hawk	8 x 8 in.	12 to 15 in.	3 in.	10 to 30 ft.

The author's experience with bluebirds indicates
that these birds often nest much nearer the ground
than five feet. They have been found nesting in
stumps but a foot or two from the ground. House
wrens, too, often nest within four feet of the ground,
and flickers at most any height. A pair of the latter
birds nested in the oak grove, in a hollow tree, and

*Farmers' Bulletin No. 609, United States Department of Agri-
culture, Washington, D. C.

Martin house.

made the entrance hole exactly three feet from the ground by actual measurement.

The entrance hole for all of the foregoing birds should be within two or three inches of the top of the front wall of the box.

The following table* gives information in regard to the shelves to be made for robins, barn swallows, and phoebes:

Name	Floor	Depth	Height
Robin	6 x 8 in.	8 in.	6 to 15 ft.
Barn swallow.................	6 x 6 in.	6 in.	8 to 12 ft.
Phoebe	6 x 6 in.	6 in.	8 to 12 ft.

There are so many things to be considered when

*Farmers' Bulletin No. 609, United States Department of Agriculture, Washington, D. C.

Nesting box for bluebirds made from part of an old,
hollow post.

building houses for martins that it is hard to handle
them by means of a table. In the first place, martins
nest in colonies, so houses made for them may have
from six to one hundred or more rooms. Each room
should measure about 6 by 6 by 6 inches on the inside, and the entrance hole should be about one inch
from the bottom of the front wall. The location of
the house also is very important, as martins are not
likely to nest in houses located near buildings and
trees or placed near the ground. The house should
be securely fastened to the top of a tall pole at least
15 feet from the ground, and the pole should stand
in the open, 50 feet or more from the nearest trees

and buildings. It also is a good idea to provide martin houses with porches for the birds to perch on.

Shelves for robins, phoebes, and barn swallows should be made from old weather-beaten boards if possible, or, if made from new lumber, should be painted a dull green or some other neutral color. The shelves should be open on two or three sides and should have roofs that will protect them from the rain. Better still, shelves for these birds may be made from slabs. Robins especially are likely to choose slab shelves in preference to board shelves, because they often nest on the branches of trees, and slabs are more like branches. The older and more weather-beaten the slabs may be, the better.

Attractive, useful, and serviceable nesting boxes may be made from lumber, but the best boxes for attracting birds which habitually nest in holes in trees, stubs, and posts are easily secured and may be made in another way. Since wrens, bluebirds, chickadees, nuthatches, tree swallows, and woodpeckers nest in hollow trees and stubs, one may easily attract and provide them with nesting sites by preparing boxes which are similar to these objects. Many people hollow out branches and tree trunks and thus prepare nesting boxes for these birds.

The author, however, has found that an easier way of securing such nesting places is to be on the lookout for hollow posts, tree trunks, branches, and stubs. There are so many of these to be found wherever trees grow that any extended walk results in the finding of one or more of them. Whenever one is found, it should be taken as a prospective house for birds. Hollow trees, stubs, and posts are sooner or later

destroyed or used for fuel, and so the taking and saving of the hollow portion is a t r u e conservation measure. When a suitable piece is found, cut it in two just above the entrance hole and then fifteen to twenty inches farther down and you have enough of it to make an attractive bird box. Take it home and fasten it to a tree or post near the house and you should have little

Another bluebird box made from a piece of post.

trouble securing feathered tenants for it. If your piece is open above, nail a board over the top and thus give it a roof; and if it is open below, nail a board over the bottom for a floor.

Sometimes large hollow tree trunks may be made to yield two such boxes. Split the hollow piece with a saw, fit a board over the back of each half, provide each with a roof and floor if necessary, and make an entrance hole for the part which has none. The entrance hole, naturally, must be made either large or small, the size depending upon the bird for which you think the finished structure is suited, or the bird you hope to attract and help by means of it.

Bird boxes made from slabs are better than bird boxes made from lumber, because slabs make the

Wren box made from a small piece cut from the trunk of a birch.

houses look more like natural nesting places in which the birds habitually nest. Other ways of making boxes more attractive to the birds are to cover them with bark and twigs, or to make them out of these materials entirely. If small branches or twigs are split with a saw and cut out into suitable lengths the pieces thus secured may be nailed to the outside of a box, where they not only add to the appearance of the structure but also give it a natural look that appeals to the birds. Bird houses, and good ones, may be made from bark, provided it is thick and tough and not likely to break, as for instance, birch bark. Boxes made from bark alone are not as durable as those made from lumber and covered with bark.

The possibilities are many, so work out something that is original and which expresses the ideas you

Bark-covered nesting box
for bluebirds.

have, and the chances are you will be rewarded for your work by securing birds for tenants. And more pleasant, helpful, and inspiring tenants are hard to imagine.

Robins have nested for years in the grape and ivy vines clinging to our west porch.

Chapter VIII

BIRDS AT NESTING TIME

THE first nesting box I ever made for bluebirds was made of some old weather-beaten boards. It was regulation style and measured five by five by seven inches on the inside and had an entrance hole one and one-half inches in diameter. I fastened this to a black oak, six feet from the ground, facing the south, where it could easily be seen and found by the birds. There were many bluebirds in the neighborhood; early in March they usually returned, hunted food in the pasture, yard, and grove, uttered their mellow, flutelike *"tur-wee,"* or *"teer-a-lee,"* courted, nested, visited our birdbath, and stayed with us until November. But though they sometimes visited my box and carefully inspected it, they never nested in it, because, no doubt, they decided it was not the kind of house they were looking for, or at least not as good as others to be found in the neighborhood. After the nesting season I saw many small flocks, or family parties, of bluebirds, composed of a pair of adult birds and from three to five youngsters, which indicated that many of their nesting ventures were successful; and each year I found many nests in hollow stumps, trees, posts, and branches. I gazed with delight at the pretty eggs, photographed many of the young and adult birds, but failed to make any impression on them as a possible bluebird landlord.

However, I did not become discouraged, hoping eventually to hit upon some type of house that would enable me to attract these pretty and useful birds to the yard. One day I noticed an old hollow fence post that had outlived its usefulness and which to all appearances had recently been used by bluebirds for nesting purposes, since it held a nest in fairly good condition. If bluebirds had nested in the old post once, why should they not nest in it again! I sawed a piece off just above the entrance hole and again sixteen inches farther down, thus securing the hollow part which I intended using as a bluebird box. I nailed some small pieces of lumber over the top and bottom, for a roof and floor, respectively, and fastened it to a post in the north fence. That same year a pair of bluebirds nested in it.

Their nesting venture was not an unqualified suc-

Flickers yearly nest in some old crippled trees I leave standing
for their use.

cess, because the birds, and their nest, were discovered by a boy who lived in the neighborhood, who
made it a practice to stop at the box whenever he
came near it. Not only did he visit it himself but he
often brought other children, much to the annoyance
of the parent bluebirds. Since the post to which the
box was fastened was on the line fence, I could
hardly object, so moved the box as soon as the young
birds were safely out of it, this time fastening it to a
bur oak south of the house. There, too, the bluebirds
found and used it, raising two broods in it, but losing
one batch of eggs when the horse rubbed himself

against the tree and knocked the box to the ground. That taught me a lesson, and I changed the pasture, so that the horse could no longer get near the box.

In the meantime I found another hollow fence post in the west fence in which bluebirds also had nested previously. The entrance hole was within a few inches of the top, so I secured an excellent box by making one cut with the saw, taking a piece about sixteen inches long from the top of the post. I nailed a thin piece of lumber over the top and another over the bottom, since the piece was open at both ends, thus giving it a roof and a floor. Then I fastened it to a post a little over a rod from the northeast corner of the house. Since then our bluebird neighbors have used this box each year, usually for two broods. I have not kept a record of the young bluebirds reared in this box, but I am sure there must have been more than thirty — and not a tragedy has occurred to mar its record.

Later I made a third box of this kind from a hollow branch, which also has been used several times by these pretty birds. Tragedy overtook a brood of young bluebirds in this box last summer. Something happened to the mother about the time the eggs hatched, and before I discovered that she was missing all her young ones were dead. This bluebird used the favorite box for her first brood, but for some reason chose another for her second. Later, the male found a new mate, this pair also using the branch box for their nest and also being doomed to failure, since the eggs for some reason failed to hatch, though the mother sat on them until late in August.

I have often placed blinds near the nests of our bluebirds in order to study their feeding habits from them, keeping records of when they began feeding the young in the morning, when they ceased at night, the number of trips made per hour, and the insects brought to the nest. Briefly, here is what I have learned in regard to our pretty and useful neighbors:

1. In May and June, bluebirds feed their young from daylight to dark, beginning at about 4:30 A.M., and continuing until late in the afternoon and sometimes until 7:30 in the evening, making from 200 to 225 trips in a day.

2. During the same months they feed their young large numbers of cutworms and later in the season many grasshoppers.

3. By estimate, when the cutworm season is at its height, these birds feed as many as 150 of the pests to their young in a day.

4. Bluebirds are among our most valuable birds because of the cutworms and grasshoppers alone which they destroy. They never do the least bit of harm.

5. Both parents help feed the young and they defend their nests with vigor.

I watched the mother feeding her young for four hours one day, my record showing that she made 51 trips to the nest with food during the time. She often went directly to her nest with the food, keeping her back turned toward me so I could not see what she had, while at other times she perched near the entrance hole and looked my way so I could see what

Bluebird at entrance hole to the first box I made from
a piece of post.

she carried in her bill. Twenty-eight times I was able
to see what she had, but twenty-three times I could
not. Eighteen of the twenty-eight times she carried
cutworms.

Next to the bluebirds the robins have been our
most confiding and interesting bird neighbors at
nesting time. Some of these birds have nested yearly
for the past seven or eight years in the grape and
ivy vines clinging to our west porch. The first year
they nested where the mother had a hard time making the grass and feathers she was using stay in
place. Some of the material fell to the ground, while
the rest was carried off by the wind. To help her, we

placed string, yarn, and the like on the ground where she would be sure to see them. In a short while she began to use these materials and made her nest almost entirely from them.

Robins carry nesting material in their bills, but after getting it to the nest, they drop or lay it down, hop upon it, work their feet rapidly and thus wedge it tightly in place; at the same time they turn this way and that, squat low or snuggle down upon it and thus shape the nest to their bodies. In other words, much of the actual work of making the nest is done with the feet, not with the bill. One year one of our robins took a bath, then wallowed in the dust and dirt in a corner of the yard and thus made mud for the main part of her nest.

The story of the nesting ventures of our robins is a long one and I can but give a few of the more important facts here. One pair built a nest in the grape vine a foot or so from the porch door, and eventually the mother became so tame that I was able to touch her when she visited the cradle with food for the young robins. On the other hand, some of them remain shy all the while they are with us, chirping anxiously whenever we get near their nests, dashing away, scolding, sputtering, and making a great deal of noise instead of remaining and keeping the eggs warm.

Two times our robins have used the same nest for two broods, once for two broods in a single season, just repairing the old nest instead of going to the trouble of building a new one.

I often fed the young birds of one brood, offering them cutworms and earthworms. At first I just touched their bills with the worm but noticed that they did not get the idea at all, sitting with their mouths as wide open as before I offered them the tidbit, not taking it and eating it as I surely thought they would. In order to get them to eat it I found that I had to push the worm far down their throats with my finger. And whenever I poked worms down their throats they closed their bills and tried their best to swallow my finger as well as the worm.

The mother robin does most of the nest building, although the male sometimes brings a few blades of dry grass, twigs, string, and feathers for her to work into the nest with her feet. Generally he just drops these into the nest, then flies off for more, but sometimes he stupidly lays them on her back. To all appearances, he knows enough to gather the different materials but not enough to actually work them into the nest. However, he does his share of the feeding, unless he is unable to get to the nest, as was the case with the male last spring. The female, then, built her nest in the thickest part of our grape vine and had a special route which enabled her to reach it with ease. The male never went near the nest until it held young birds, and then he tried to reach it by an almost impossible way through a heavy part of the vine.

Three times robins have nested on robin shelves I made for them. These shelves were made according to the specifications given in the preceding chap-

Robins sometimes nest on the shelves I make for them.

ter and were fastened to the barn and henhouse, the one on the barn being used twice and the other once. And all three ventures were successful.

Young trees are used most freely by our robin neighbors when nesting (especially oaks, box elders, and elms) and the birds nearly always build their cradles in suitable crotches and rather near the ground. Vines come second in popularity, the branches of large trees third, and ledges and shelves next. And these birds are most confiding, choosing places within a short distance of the house for practically all their nests. This is partly due to the fact that the most suitable vines and trees are located near the house, but robins also seem to understand that they are safest when nesting near us, since enemies of various kinds dare not molest them. And, of course, one of the chief reasons why most people love and protect the robin is due to the fact that it is confiding and is perhaps better known than any other bird.

Our robins always build a half dozen nests they never use for one reason or another, no doubt in most instances deciding after building them that they do not like their locations. Many nests are ruined by the rain, or strong winds, or are visited by gray squirrels, of which there are many in the neighborhood.

Robins are not as useful as bluebirds, because they eat many strawberries, cherries, and raspberries while they remain with us. Not only do the adult birds live largely upon berries when they are to be had, but they feed many of them to their young.

One cannot write about attracting birds by means of bird boxes without mentioning the house wren. In the country, these birds nest in holes in trees, stumps, and posts. In cities and villages they find boxes and all sorts of other odd places. Any extended walk along the streets of cities and villages usually results in the seeing of several of them. They are to be heard singing, and to be seen bobbing and flitting about boxes fastened to buildings and trees. Sometimes the house to which a pair has taken a fancy is fastened to the branch of a tree with a wire, and swings gently back and forth in every slightest breeze. They

Bluebird at the favorite box. She has a cutworm for her young.

frequently are to be seen in unusual places, such as dump heaps, for example, carrying twigs and weed stalks into tin cans, boxes, bags, and what not.

My experience with wrens has been much like that with bluebirds. The first ones to nest on the premises built their cradle in the south wall of the henhouse. They entered through a knothole, and built the nest in some straw used for insulating purposes. Thereafter, for several years, they nested elsewhere, although they frequently visited us for a few days, carefully inspected everything, lugged twigs into our wren houses, sang, and bustled about. Eventually they left, as much as to say: *"We've looked over what you have to offer, but do not find anything that quite suits us. We'll call again later, and may stay, if you have a box we like better."*

I finally made a wren box out of a hollow piece of birch. The hollow portion was eight inches long. I split it, fastened half of it to a board, gave it a roof and floor, and bored a hole in it an inch in diameter. (See illustration, page 70.) Since then I have had no trouble inducing these birds to nest near us.

We also have a good many flickers and red-headed woodpeckers nesting near us each year. I have some hollow-post and hollow-branch boxes large enough to accommodate these birds, but they never use them, preferring to nest in hollow trees instead. And I always leave a few old hollow trees standing in the grove and pasture for them. Old dead, partly decayed, or hollow trees are worth ten healthy young trees for attracting birds, so a few of them should be left standing.

A pair of tree swallows and a pair of nuthatches also have nested on our grounds, the tree swallows building their cradle in a hollow post in the west fence, and the nuthatches choosing a hollow bur oak in the pasture. The swallows lost all but one of their youngsters through a mishap. The post they chose was old and decayed. At first the young birds had plenty of room in the cavity, but they grew rapidly and soon found their quarters hot and crowded. They squirmed and jostled each other about, broke the outer wall from their home, and fell to the ground; that is, all but one of them. I saved the life of the lone survivor by tying the piece of post securely back in place with a strong piece of string.

Wild crab tree.

Chapter IX

TREES, BUSHES, VINES, AND FLOWERS

TREES, bushes, and vines do more to attract birds than birdbaths, food trays, and nesting boxes. The planting of them is the most important consideration for the bird lover and prospective bird landlord to take into account. If you have a bird sanctuary, no matter how small, even though it be but a part of the back yard, you will have some bird neighbors, if it has some trees and shrubs. Many birds will visit you in order to feed on the insect pests to be found about the plants; they will use the plants for shelter during storms, for protection from the heat of the sun, and for roosting and nesting purposes; and

85

about them they will flit and dart, sing, court, and
seek protection from their enemies. Birds of many
species will be attracted by trees and bushes whether
you have any birdbaths, food trays, and nesting
boxes or not.

Birds are fond of all trees, and the two go naturally
together. Were all our trees destroyed, many birds,
no doubt, would perish with them, although some
might get along very well, and others would be able
to adjust their lives accordingly. Wild ducks and
other waterfowl, bobolinks, and chimney swifts might
get along rather well, but what about the woodpeckers, chickadees, nuthatches, brown creepers,
orioles, vireos, and warblers?

Secure a tree guide, look through it page by page,
notice the names of the trees, the number of different
species, and then remember that all of them are useful for attracting birds. A bird can use any tree, no
matter how dwarfed and humble, for roosting purposes, shelter, protection from enemies, and for securing part of its food supply. However, some trees are
more valuable for attracting birds than others, since
some of them bear berries, others nuts and seeds, and
still others fruit of various kinds. Maple, ash, and
many other trees produce seeds for the birds to eat.
The hackberry, Russian mulberry, and Juneberry
produce berries our feathered friends and neighbors
take in large numbers; and the red, choke, and black
cherries also provide many of them with food. Plum,
thorn, and crabapple trees produce fruits that are
relished by birds. Other trees attract birds by their
sap, as, for example, the maple, which the yellow-

A wonderful place for birds. The tree near the center is a
wild thorn, that in the right background an elm.

bellied sapsucker often visits when he is thirsty and
wishes a drink; the catalpa appeals to others because
of its flowers, since some species are able to find insects about the blossoms; and the oaks are loved by
the red-headed woodpecker who lives largely on
acorns in winter.

The cottonwood, box elder, and American elm are
very valuable trees for attracting birds. This may
sound strange to people who are accustomed to think
of the box elder and cottonwood as being undesirable for various reasons. The reasons I value these
trees are because they are easy to make grow and
grow rapidly. Suppose, for example, to make my

point clear, that you built a house on a plot of ground on which there were no trees and the soil poor, and suppose that you wished to make the place attractive both to yourself and the birds as soon as possible, what trees would you plant, first of all? Now you can have large trees planted there at once, but this is very expensive. Shrubbery and flowers can transform a barren piece of ground to an attractive place almost overnight. But suppose, on the other hand, that you have little money to spend on trees and bushes, then you will be obliged to go at the matter in an entirely different way. In this book, as elsewhere stated, we are not concerned with things that cost a great deal or which are hard to make. The birdbaths previously described may be made at little or no cost; the same is true of the feeding devices and nesting boxes. But, though we are concerned with simple devices which may be made in the cheapest possible way, common trees, bushes, and vines, wholesome and cheap foods, and humble yards, remember these may be used to attract birds to splendid advantage, almost as effectively as costly and elaborate devices, dainty foods, costly plantings, and parklike grounds.

The box elder is considered to be an undesirable tree by many people because it attracts insects. However, the bird lover and bird landlord should never overlook the fact that trees and other plants which attract insects also attract the birds. I find the box elder to be both interesting and valuable and that it is easy to plant and grows rapidly and its branches spread freely. You can plant a box elder and be quite

Crippled and partly dead trees attract many birds.

sure it will grow and that in a few years it will be large enough to prove attractive to the birds. If squirrels are about, this tree produces seeds which they like. Each year gray squirrels come to our yard, where they feed on the seeds of our box elders.

The cottonwood is valuable and worth having for much the same reasons as the box elder.

The American elm is even more desirable than the box elder and cottonwood, since it not only is easy to make grow and grows rapidly but also has an attractive, fan-shaped head or crown and pretty leaves and branches. To be sure, there are other trees having the same qualities, that may be planted at the start. They may be used to attract birds until the more desirable ones attain enough growth to take their places. This, then, is the idea: plant sure-growing and rapidly growing trees at first, even though you do not like them, or think them undesirable, until you have raised enough desirable ones to take their places; then cut the former.

Old, crippled, and partly dead and decayed trees are, as a rule, better for attracting birds than young, healthy ones. Birds which nest in holes in trees make their cradles in dead and partly decayed trunks and branches in preference to sound ones. Willow trees, I find, are highly prized by house wrens, bluebirds, tree swallows, and woodpeckers. A near-by stream has many willows growing along its banks, in which large numbers of these birds nest. Indeed, it is almost impossible to find a willow of any size and age which has not one or more holes in it, and which has not at one time or another been used by birds for nesting purposes. While young willows are tough and pliable, old willows are just the reverse, breaking easily and presenting a crippled appearance. The wood of the willow is soft and light, decays rapidly, and soon becomes so brittle that tree swallows, house wrens, and bluebirds are able to make holes in it. These birds, however, generally leave the drilling of holes to the woodpeckers, who hollow out suitable nesting sites with ease. Willows also are often crooked and deformed and have natural holes, cracks, and crevices in them.

Nor are willows the only trees that appeal to the aforementioned birds. The same is true of the red birch, canoe birch, and poplars or aspens. The wood of birches is harder than that of willows, but it decays rapidly, much faster than the bark, and birches are rather easily killed and broken. Poplars have soft, light wood which breaks easily. Take a walk to a poplar grove and you will be sure to see many that are dead or partly decayed, some lying on the ground, others leaning heavily upon their neighbors, and still others standing but so far gone that you can push them over with ease. Or, take a walk through a birch grove and you are likely to find many that are dead or crippled. Here is one with a dead top, there another with a large dead branch, and yonder one that is broken in the middle. Birch stubs with several holes in them are easy to find. Trees, then, which have soft wood, are easily broken, and killed, and which decay rapidly are liked by many birds.

From what has been said in the preceding paragraph, it is a mistake to cut your old and crippled trees and to have only young, healthy ones if you are interested in having the greatest possible number of birds for neighbors. As pointed out in a previous chapter, I have flickers and red-headed woodpeckers for neighbors during the nesting season because I have some old hollow oaks about the place. I have never cut these trees for fuel because I wished to attract woodpeckers by means of them.

How valuable old crippled trees are for attracting birds is well illustrated by a crippled elm I often pass in a neighbor's front yard, when on my way to the

A bushy wild thorn in which both catbirds and brown
thrashers have nested.

store or post office. It has a dead top and in this are
at least two large woodpeckers' holes. I chanced to
pass this tree one day, last winter, and found four
species of birds in it, sputtering and quarreling over
them. Each wished to gain possession and hold them
against all comers, because they would furnish
them storage room, sleeping quarters, and part of
their food supply. Only the birds knew how snug
and warm the holes were on cold winter nights, what
treasures they held, and what insects and other pests
they harbored. The brown creeper, downy woodpecker, and the chickadee habitually get all or part of
their food supply from just such trees, and also nest
or sleep in holes in them. The present winter I have
kept a close watch over this tree and have seldom

passed it without finding such birds as English sparrows, blue jays, nuthatches, chickadees, woodpeckers, and others about it. No other tree that I know does more to attract birds, no other tree is more interesting, and no other yard proves better for the study and observation of birds than the one in which this crippled elm stands.

Trees with dense, bushy tops or which spread rapidly and form thickets are also liked by the birds. Good examples of such trees are the wild crab, wild plum, wild thorn, river birch, willow, and the black locust.

The fragrant and prairie crabs are small trees with dense spreading tops. They are armed with short, sharp spurs which make them hard and disagreeable for people to climb and cause cattle and other animals to avoid them, or at least to be careful when near them. They have many crooked branches, numerous tough, leafy twigs, and many tangled, sheltered crotches that make ideal nesting places for robins, blue jays, thrashers, and catbirds. Often they are bushes and not trees, densely tangled affairs armed with sharp spurs, and are then doubly attractive to the birds. The only cedar waxwing's nest I ever found had been built in a small, bushy, wildcrab tree.

What has been said of the wild crabs is equally true of the various wild thorns. Wild thorns are about as large as wild crabs, have the same dense, spreading tops, and often are large bushes, not trees, armed with long, smooth, sharp needles. Often thorn bushes are so dense and thickly covered with leaves that their branches, twigs, thorns, and any nests they may hold are hidden from view. Little wonder the birds find them ideal for nesting purposes, because enemies have trouble seeing and finding the cradles in the first place and are not able to reach them when they do. Catbirds, robins, brown thrashers, and many other birds make good use of thorn trees and bushes when nesting.

Wild-plum trees resemble wild crabs and thorns in many ways. They vary in size and are likely to have branches by the score, and be surrounded by any number of smaller plum trees. Consequently they are often found growing in thickets, and thickets always prove attractive to birds of many species. Plum trees are protected by sharp twigs, not spurs and needles like the crabs and thorns.

Wild crabs, wild thorns, and wild plums are rather easy to make grow. Then, too, all of them produce fruit the birds can use for food. To be sure, the birds are not as fond of wild crabs, thorn apples, and plums as they are of cherries and a dozen other kinds of wild berries that might be mentioned, but when hard pressed for food they are likely to eat them. Thorn apples, no doubt, are eaten more freely than wild crabs and wild plums, since they are much smaller and hold many large seeds. Many of them are wormy and for this reason appeal to birds that live on an insect diet. The ruffed grouse and nearly a dozen other birds are known to eat thorn apples. Taken as a whole, there are few trees that are any better for attracting birds than wild crabs, wild thorns, and wild plums, so the bird lover should, if possible, plant

Blue jay on nest in wild thorn.

some of them, or, if he already has some on the
premises should spare them in preference to others.

The red or river birch, naturally tall and slender,
is often found in colonies along streams and near
lakes and ponds. About a mile west of my home
flows a tributary of the Mississippi River, and on a
point between the main channel and an adjoining
slough is a large red-birch thicket, consisting of all
young trees about the same age and size, and their
small lower branches are all dead from lack of sunshine. These tiny dead branches are on a level with
one's face and make the walking difficult. But the
birds like this thicket because it is so dense, inacces-
sible to enemies, and near to water. In it, each year,
many green herons, catbirds, yellow warblers, cuck-

oos, and other birds nest. About its borders are to be found the nests of red-winged blackbirds, mourning doves, wood thrushes, grackles, vireos, warblers, house wrens, tree swallows, and others.

Willows, too, very frequently are to be found in dense thickets along the banks of streams and other places near water, and are freely used by the same species of birds. They also are easy to plant, especially in places where there is plenty of moisture in the soil. Sharpen a twig or branch and run it into the soil, or break off a branch and cover the butt end with soil, and most likely it will take root.

Oak trees are liked rather well by some birds when nesting. In this neighborhood robins, blue jays, crows, brown thrashers, flickers, red-headed woodpeckers, mourning doves, vireos, and orioles use them for nesting purposes. Black and bur oaks usually have dead branches, and many of them are hollow. Occasionally a dead branch breaks off and falls to the ground, thus providing a woodpecker with a suitable place to drill a home. The red-headed woodpecker likes the oak tree best of all. It not only nests in holes it drills in oaks, but also it spends the nights in them. It hunts insect pests about their trunks and branches and eats large quantities of acorns. This bird is as fond of and dependent upon the oaks as gray and fox squirrels. Where there are no oaks you will find few squirrels, unless there are nut trees of various other kinds to take their places, and where there are no oaks you will find few red-headed woodpeckers. This woodpecker lives on insects and other small creatures in summer, which it gleans from the trunks and branches of trees in true woodpecker style, or catches on the wing much like the flycatchers, but as soon as the acorns are ripe it eats many of them and devotes most of its time to gathering and storing them for the coming winter.

Wild cherry trees, especially the red, black, and choke cherries, are favorites with the birds. They not only attract them but also furnish part of their food supply. Red cherries are prime favorites and the birds eat them about as fast as they ripen. They are bright-red when ripe and smaller than choke or black cherries. The trees usually are small, though they have been known to attain a height of forty feet and to have trunks a foot in diameter.

The choke cherry is smaller than the red-cherry tree, often being a bush instead of a tree. But it has the most attractive flowers, which are pure-white and found in thick, cylindrical clusters known as racemes. The cherries are very sour and bitter and not fit to eat until fully ripe. Then they are sometimes used for making jellies and pies, or are eaten raw. We used to gather them, put them in a glass, add sugar, and a pinch of salt, shake them well, and then eat them. But we never ate many, finding them little to our taste. Then, too, we were told that people, children especially, often choked to death if they ate many of them or drank milk after so doing. Choke cherries are about a third of an inch in diameter and are found in attractive clusters or bunches.

The black cherry is the largest and most valuable of the wild cherries, sometimes attaining a height of eighty feet and having a trunk three feet in diameter.

A small wild-plum thicket.

However, if you find one that has a trunk a foot or more in diameter, it may be considered comparatively large. The wood has a rich brown color, makes excellent lumber, and is very valuable. The cherries are about as large as choke cherries and are used for making jellies and pies. The birds like all of our wild cherries. Robins, cedar waxwings, and a few others live largely on them when they are in season.

Evergreens are attractive to many birds, furnishing them with nesting and roosting places and part of their food supply. The pine, spruce, hemlock, fir, cedar, and juniper are all evergreens that appeal to birds for various reasons. Nearly all of them produce seeds which are freely eaten by many species. Pine grosbeaks and crossbills feed on the seeds of pines, and birds of a dozen or more species are known to eat the bluish-white berries of the red cedar. Ten or more species eat the light-blue berries of the common juniper, the most widely distributed tree of the northern hemisphere. Many birds habitually roost in evergreens, as these trees protect them from the cold, snow, strong winds, and enemies. Some evergreens are freely used for hedges and windbreaks and incidentally help and attract birds at the same time. That these trees appeal strongly to some birds is proved by the fact that some species are only to be found in neighborhoods where evergreens are numerous.

The mountain ash, both the American or small-fruited, and the large-fruited, are small and have compound leaves, clusters of small flowers, and attractive bunches of red berries. Bluebirds, robins, flickers, grosbeaks, purple finches, white-throated sparrows, downy woodpeckers, and so on, are known to eat their berries.

The bayberry or wax myrtle is a diminutive but favorite tree which produces small berries which are coated with a light-blue wax, hence the name, wax myrtle. They are eaten by fifteen or more species of birds. The myrtle warbler gets its name from this tree, of whose berries it is very fond, remaining in the North as long as they are plentiful.

The fruit of the flowering dogwood also is prized by many birds, thirty or more species being known to eat it. So too are the fruits of the staghorn sumac, black haw, and nannyberries. The former is the small tree with staglike twigs and branches, scarlet autumn leaves, and panicles of red berry-like drupes. The black haw and nannyberries are useful and interesting chiefly because of their berries, that are freely eaten both by children and birds and are often called wild raisins. The berries are bitter until fully ripe, and the flat seeds are so large that there is little else to them. These trees are about as large as the red and choke cherry, and they have many shrubby relatives, such as the high-bush cranberry, arrowwood, hobble bush, and dockmackie.

Three important trees, which appeal to the birds because of the berries they produce, remain to be considered: the Juneberry, mulberry, and hackberry.

The Juneberry, also known as the serviceberry, shad-blow, and shadbush, is a small tree thirty, forty, or fifty feet tall which may have a trunk a foot or so in diameter. It is very beautiful in mid-spring when in full bloom; its blossoms are pure-white and found in pretty nodding racemes. The berries are about as large as choke cherries and are very delicious, ripening in June and July and being taken almost at once by the birds.

We have two mulberries, both of which are popular with the birds, more than thirty species being known to eat their fruit. In shape the berries are much like a blackberry or dewberry. These are the red and white mulberries, the former being a native and the latter an introduced tree. Mulberry seedlings may be purchased from nurseries for a few cents each. Many of them are set out yearly by people who are interested in attracting and helping the birds.

A veteran wild black-cherry tree.

The hackberry is the largest and most stately of all berry-producing trees, sometimes getting to be one hundred feet in height and having a trunk five feet in diameter. In size and shape it resembles the American elm, being one of the tallest and most stately trees known. It may be distinguished from the elm by its grayish bark which is furrowed and more or less covered with warty growths. The leaves are long and tapering and have pointed tips, toothed edges, and three main veins. The berries are about as large as black or choke cherries and are purple in color when ripe. They have long threadlike stems and are suspended singly beneath the leaves. The berries are conspicuous after the leaves have fallen, clinging to the trees much of the winter if not eaten meanwhile by the birds. Where hackberry trees are numerous, even in our most northern states, robins are likely to remain all winter long; and cardinals, cedar waxwings, and many other birds eat quantities of their sweet berries.

All bushes, whether wild, tame, or purely ornamental, though those which produce berries or other fruit are by far the best, also prove attractive to the birds. Spirea, barberry, rose, currant, gooseberry, raspberry, blackberry, and lilac are the most common. Bushes furnish birds with nesting places, shelter from the elements and enemies, and part of their food. Currants, gooseberries, and blackberries are very good, and raspberries even better. While birds like blackberries for food, they are not likely to use many of the canes or vines for nesting purposes, since there is little for them to fasten their cradles to.

The author feels that the raspberry bush is the most excellent for attracting birds. The tame red and black raspberries attract birds by their berries, have neat ornamental canes, and are used freely at nesting time. The wild black raspberry is even better, since the birds find its berries delicious, and its plumelike canes attractive. What wonderful thickets

The pretty blossoms of the black haw.

these plants form! What wonderful nesting places they afford!

Two vines, it seems, are especially valuable for attracting birds: the five-leaved ivy or Virginia creeper, and the wild grape. Both of these vines are very common, easily secured, and produce fruit the birds like. They also provide excellent nesting places, and are easy to make grow. Wild grapes are to be found mainly along roadsides, streams, and in pastures, while the five-leaved ivy is to be found cropping out along fence rows, in waste places, about the edges of fields, and along highways. Plants of both species in large numbers usually may be had for the asking. They may be planted along foundations, about porches, in corners of the yard, and in front of trellises. Some may prefer to train them up the sides of the house or porch, and up trees and bushes.

Flowers may and should be planted to attract two of our most interesting birds: the ruby-throated hummingbird and the goldfinch. The goldfinch will visit cosmos, sunflowers, and other species for their seeds, while the hummingbird will visit many for their nectar.

The person wishing to attract birds in the largest numbers should plan on having a thicket or two. Catbirds and brown thrashers are fond of them when nesting; so, too, are the chipping and field sparrows. Juncos and tree sparrows are sure to visit them in winter, and birds of a dozen species during the spring and autumn migrations.

The thickets should contain berry trees, nut trees, box elders, elms, birches, cottonwoods, raspberry bushes, ivy vines, and wild grapes. They should be located in a corner of the yard, about a pool, or on the south side of a grove of trees. At the same time they may be made to serve as a windbreak for the house and food tray. In summer, naturally, they may furnish shade for birdbaths; and all of them tend to make the yard and its surroundings more attractive.

Chipping sparrow on nest brooding her young.

Chapter X

HELPING BIRDS AT NESTING TIME

TWO of our most interesting and useful bird neighbors have been the chipping and field sparrows, which have been attracted to our yard and sanctuary by thickets and bushes. These birds like to hunt insects and other foods and to build their nests in bushes and vines, although the field sparrow also at times nests on the ground in a tuft of weeds, grass, or brush. Both are a little over five inches in length and have long tails and brownish crowns. The field sparrow has a pink bill, and this is the mark by means of which it may at once be identified. It has a light-brown crown, and a brownish wash on the sides. The chipping sparrow has a chestnut crown, black forehead, and light lines above the eyes. Black lines also extend back across the eyes.

The field sparrow has much the sweeter and more interesting song; this is likely to be heard at any time of the day or night. It is a loud, clear whistle which can be heard for a long distance, and usually it is rather short and simple, the latter notes being uttered much faster than the first. This bird often sings a long and varied song which sounds unlike the common and more simple one. Its inspired song is to be heard at the height of the mating and nesting season, when the weather is agreeable. The song of the more confiding chipping sparrow is but the word *"chip"* repeated over and over in a long, low, drowsy series. The nests of both are made of grass and lined with hair, the chipping sparrow using much more hair than the field sparrow, so much, in fact, that it is also known as the hairbird. The chipping sparrow's eggs are among the prettiest of all birds' eggs, being light bluish-green and spotted, chiefly about the larger end, with dark-brown.

Each year a half dozen or more pairs of these birds build their nests in our bushes, and each pair usually raises at least two broods of youngsters on the premises during the season. We find a good many of the nests while they actually are in use, but some we do not find until leaves have fallen from the bushes in the fall. But whether we find the nests or not, we know exactly when the birds are nesting, since the whistled songs of the field sparrows and the

A field sparrow brooding its young — field sparrows at times seem inspired. Then their songs are so varied and out of the ordinary as to be scarcely recognizable.

drowsy *"chip-chip-chip-chip"* of the chipping sparrows are heard at all times of the day. More field sparrows than chipping sparrows nest near us.

I am very fond of the little field sparrow, my liking being chiefly due to its habit of singing at night. Its nocturnal song is very simple, yet sweet and inspiring, a single strain of tinkling music that reminds me of a musical alarm clock. The songster usually sings his little ditty when disturbed by some noise, such as the barking of a dog, the crowing of a rooster, the honking of an automobile horn, the whistling of a train, or the sound of a footstep.

Although the field sparrow has the sweeter and

more interesting song, the chipping sparrow is the more confiding and brave. One that nested in a bush near the house one year became so tame that she allowed me to touch her when she was on her nest. Another pair built their nest in the grape vine clinging to the porch. The nest was never used because a cowbird tried to lay an egg in it. I frightened the shiftless impostor from the dainty little cradle before she had time to do so. Nevertheless, the sparrows deserted it and built another nest a short distance off in a raspberry bush.

Vesper and lark sparrows build many nests about the place each year. However, there is not much one can do to attract them. They build their nests on the ground in tufts of weeds and grass, hills of corn, potatoes, and beans, and in piles of leaves and rubbish. One is likely to run across their nests on the ground most anywhere. Vesper sparrows have streaked breasts and sides, chestnut shoulders, and white outer tail feathers, the latter being their mark of identification. They sing very sweetly late in the day, and it is for this reason they are known as vesper sparrows. They are our true field sparrows, as they not only nest on the ground in fields but also spend much of their time there. The field sparrow, on the other hand, is not a field sparrow at all but a bush or pasture sparrow.

The lark sparrow is one of the prettiest of all sparrows, having alternate white and brown stripes on the sides of the head and crown, a spot on the center of the breast, and white-tipped tail feathers. When the tail is spread, as it often is, it looks like a tiny fan with a white border. Both lark and vesper sparrows have sweet and inspiring songs.

Meadowlarks also frequently nest in the grass in the immediate vicinity, and we always do our best to attract them by leaving the grass in the sanctuary uncut. These birds like to build their nests in tall, dry grass, so we never burn the dead grass, nor cut it when it is green, as so many people do, so that the meadowlark may have places to nest. Nor do we ever use our little refuge for a pasture. If you wish to have these pretty and useful birds for neighbors, leave at least part of the grass in your yard or sanctuary uncut, and do not burn it over in the spring and fall.

I studied the feeding habits of a pair of these birds that nested in our sanctuary one year and noticed that the mother did all the feeding and that she secured many cutworms for her young. She carried these destructive insects by the nape of the neck, much like a cat carries a kitten. The worms she carried always were alive and performed all sorts of gymnastic exercises in their efforts to get away. They squirmed and wiggled and described arcs with the free parts of their bodies in a very comical way. The male never helped feed the young, but he always sang freely and sweetly in the immediate vicinity of the nest; and he guarded his mate and her nest constantly, warning her when intruders were near by means of a characteristic alarm note: *"still, still, still-ll-ll-l."* Perhaps he was trying to say, or did say, *"Be still — don't move — crouch still lower — I see him — be careful."* At any rate whenever he uttered

Nest and eggs of catbird. They are interesting
neighbors of ours.

his warning *"still-ll-ll-l,"* she either remained motionless or tried her best to hide; but, when he sang his
pleasant *"spring-o'-the-year,"* she went about her
work as usual.

The catbird and brown thrasher also are common
and interesting neighbors of ours, and both are easily
attracted by means of thickets, bushes, and brush
piles. Brown thrashers have nested near the house
as long as I can remember, but the catbirds did not
until the thicket west of the house attained its present size and density. Every catbird's nest built in
our sanctuary has been built in this thicket. Catbirds
and brown thrashers are closely related; they might

be called bird cousins. Their long bills, expressive tails, and songs show their relationship. Their songs are so much alike that it sometimes is hard to tell whether a given songster is one or the other. However, the song of the thrasher is louder and richer than that of the catbird, and consists largely of couplets; while that of the catbird often is given a comical twist and may consist of snatches from the songs of a number of other species of birds. For the latter reason the catbird is also known as the northern mockingbird. The songs of both are varied. The location of the songster often is of help to one when trying to decide whether a given bird is a thrasher or catbird, the former singing from the tops of tall trees and poles and the latter from objects nearer the ground, often from tangles and bushes.

Our catbird neighbors have not been very successful when nesting, mainly because they do not seem to be able to anchor their cradles properly. On at least two occasions they have raised but one youngster, losing the other eggs or young through accidents to their nests. Several nests I have had under observation have been destroyed by the wind; others have fallen to the ground before serving the purpose for which they were built. At any rate, provide a thicket if you wish catbirds for neighbors. Catbirds often nest in bushes and small bushy trees near ponds and streams, and they are fond of water, so a birdbath always proves attractive to them. They will visit a birdbath many times a day and will entertain you with excellent music between times.

Brown thrashers not only nest in bushes and small

bushy trees, but also in brush piles, vines, and when these are not available on the lower branches of trees. I always prepared or left a few brush piles expressly for these pretty brown birds before we had many thickets and bushes in our sanctuary, and thus induced many of them, which otherwise might have gone elsewhere, to nest near us.

Brown thrashers are shrewd, secretive, and sensitive, deserting their nests if they believe their whereabouts known to other birds, or if they are visited by human beings or other intruders. Consequently, one must be careful not to frighten them, go near their nests, or touch their eggs.

> "And the brown thrush* keeps singing, 'A nest do you see,
> And five eggs hid by me in the juniper tree?
> Don't meddle! don't touch! little girl, little boy,
> Or the world will lose some of its joy!' "
> — *Lucy Larcom*

Brown thrashers, nevertheless, are brave and do their best to defend their nests after they hold young birds, sometimes attacking enemies, or other intruders, and striking them with their beaks and feet. When alarmed, they utter sharp clicking notes which are loud and out of the ordinary; then, too, they utter a whistled *"whee-u, whee-u,"* a harsh *"charr-rr-r,"* and scream and make much noise.

*The brown thrasher is sometimes called the brown thrush. This bird, however, is not a thrush at all, but is closely related to the catbird, mockingbird, and wren. Our true thrushes, and thrushlike birds, are the bluebird, robin, veery, and the hermit, gray-cheeked, and olive-backed thrushes.

Brown thrasher brooding. Thickets, bushes, and brush piles
attract these birds.

Both catbirds and brown thrashers build excellent
cradles for their eggs and young. The catbird's nest
is cup-shaped, made of twigs and weeds, and lined
with rootlets. That of the brown thrasher is made
of the same material, somewhat larger than the catbird's cradle, and is flatter, shaped much like a
saucer. The eggs of the catbird are greenish-blue,
while those of the brown thrasher are white, thickly
and evenly spotted with brown.

Each year, too, a number of blue jays nest near
the yard. These birds build their nests mostly of
twigs in trees, usually on branches or in crotches.
There is little one can do to attract them aside from
having trees to their liking. Although blue jays are
noisy, they are among the quietest of birds when

nesting, and they know how to avoid being seen and keep the locations of their nests a secret. They have many calls, alarms, and conversational notes, using the latter freely when nest building, the birds of a pair talking or communicating freely with each other. *"Tee, tee, tee,"* they often say in low tones, as much as to say: *"This is the place for our nest. Go fetch me some twigs, but be sure to be careful. None of our enemies must know we are building a nest. Tee, tee, tee—Now our nest is ready for use,"* or *"Haven't we the prettiest eggs you ever saw?"* or *"Don't you think we have cunning youngsters?"*

Young blue jays are very attractive when nearly full grown, prove excellent subjects for photographs, and are easily managed. And the parent birds love their young, are brave, and defend their nests to the best of their ability. They are shrewd, hardy and full of life and energy. How much life and color they add to our winter landscapes.

> Rains never dim his smooth blue coat,
> The winter never troubles him;
> No fog puts hoarseness in his throat
> Or makes his merry eyes grow dim.
> — *Author unknown*

We generally have one or more pairs of Baltimore orioles for neighbors, too. These birds nest near the ends of the branches of tall trees, weaving their pendant pouchlike cradle of string, yarn, and other similar materials. They may be attracted, encouraged, and helped by means of such materials; these

Nest and pure-white eggs of the bobwhite.

may be scattered over the ground, hung on branches, wires, or bushes, or left elsewhere, where the birds will have little trouble finding them.

> Hush! 'tis he!
> My Oriole, my glance of summer fire,
> Is come at last; and ever on the watch,
> Twitches the pack thread I had lightly wound
> About the bough to help his housekeeping.
> — *Lowell*

A pair of vireos, also, built their swinging cradle in the top of a bur oak south of the house. I often watched the owners at work on the nest, knew its exact location, but never attempted to climb the tree for a better look at the dainty affair. After our trees are bare of leaves in the fall, I often find the nests of vireos in them, nests I never dreamed were there, in which broods of young birds were reared without our being aware of the fact.

Several pairs of bobwhites have nested on the premises. The first nest I ever found had been built in the grass near the base of an oak in the grove, less than five rods from the house. The mother became so tame that I set the camera within four feet of her and took her picture. The male perched in a tree a rod or two off meanwhile and sang his clear whistled *"bobwhite"* or *"more-wet."* I finally frightened the mother from her nest and she walked slowly off with her eyes on the ground, uttering notes that sounded like *"un-chip-chip, um-chip-chip,"* as if to say, *"Look — look here, don't look there — if you do, you'll find my nest."*

Another pair built their nest in some tall grass along the south fence. This nest was a dome-shaped affair much like that of the meadowlark and had a large round hole in one side which served for an entrance. This nest had four eggs in it the day I found it; later others were laid until there were eight in all. Then the eggs began to disappear one by one until there were but four left. I am quite sure that the mother deserted this nest because I was obliged to work near it, and either carried off or destroyed the missing eggs.

Sometimes I run across broods of young bobwhites in the weeds and grass. The little fellows look like brown-leghorn chicks and are able to run surprisingly fast, dashing this way and that, hiding in the weeds and grass, and are hard to catch. After they have taken refuge in what they consider a safe place, they

Adult nighthawk resting.

sit as still as only frightened baby bobwhites know
how to sit and are almost impossible to find. And you
can step on them without causing them to cry out.
The eggs are pure-white, and there are from eight
or ten to eighteen or more of them in a clutch. Leaving the grass in the sanctuary uncut is perhaps the
only thing one can do to attract and help bobwhites
at nesting time. If the birds are fed in the neighborhood in winter, they are more likely to nest near you
than if you allow them to shift for themselves.

The nighthawk is an interesting bird neighbor of
ours, although it is not attracted to the premises by
anything we do. It just happens to come, that's all
there is to it, a fact, however, which pleases us and
affords us considerable enjoyment, since it is such
a queer bird and such a wonderful flyer. This bird
nests on the bare ground, laying a pair of mottled

eggs among the chips and bark, on a suitable bare spot, or the ashes left by a recent fire. The bird feigns injury when you get near its eggs or young, spreading its wings, gasping, and fluttering about on the ground near you. Walk toward it and it flutters off a few feet and repeats the performance. Sometimes one says rather plainly, *"quit."* Perhaps that is exactly the idea the fluttering, gasping bird desires to express. *"Quit — quit following me. Please leave before you find or step on my precious eggs or young."* Nighthawks differ from most birds in perching lengthwise on the branches of trees, not crosswise. Their flight is interesting and marvelous. They fly during the morning and evening hours mainly, and on dark cloudy days and moonlight nights, and remain on the wing for long periods of time. Often one flies upward a step at a time, first flapping its wings, then holding them motionless, until it is high in the sky, when it turns and shoots rapidly toward the ground. All at once it turns sharply and you hear a loud booming or zooming sound which is made by the air as it rushes swiftly by or through the stiff wing feathers. The nighthawk is wooing a mate when thus engaged, its flight and booming corresponding to the drumming, strutting, displaying and singing of other birds. The bird secures all its food from the atmosphere, overtaking, catching, and eating all sorts of winged pests as it flies about.

The bird landlord should act in such a way that the birds realize he is a friend wishing them only good and not harm. The young bird is a red-headed woodpecker.

Chapter XI

PROTECTING YOUR BIRD NEIGHBORS

BIRDS not only have many enemies, but they also die from disease, lose their lives through accidents of various kinds, and have other troubles, so the person who is interested in them and wishes them for neighbors must continually be ready to help and protect them. He must know how to help injured birds, how to feed starving nestlings, what enemies prey upon them, how to protect them to the best advantage from these enemies, how to act when near their nests, together with many other things.

119

The bird lover and bird landlord should at all times act in such a way that the birds realize he is a friend wishing them only good and not harm. It is a good plan to walk or move about slowly when near them, to talk to them perhaps, and to sit still for long periods of time watching them. Though it sometimes is permissible to play, run, laugh, talk, and shout in the sanctuary, there are times when one should avoid doing some of these things. I have noticed that many birds are sensitive to sudden noises, some of those feeding on our food tray dashing headlong from it when a door slams or anything else makes a loud noise. Sudden movements near them also cause them to dash off. If a person is good at imitating their songs and calls, he often is able to get near them and win their confidence by means of the accomplishment.

The best way to make the birds living near you comfortable is to pay little attention to them. If they realize that you are watching them they become suspicious. This was well illustrated by a robin that nested in one of our grape vines one spring. We were sitting on the front steps one day talking, less than six feet from the mother, who was on the nest. So long as we only sat there and talked the bird paid no attention to us. Finally I turned and looked squarely at her, then she at once became uneasy and flew off. So long as you go about your daily tasks in your usual way you are not likely to alarm the birds, but go near them, watch them, meddle with their affairs, and you frighten them. A bird sanctuary is not the proper place for baseball or other games in which there is much running, shouting, and excitement. And the bird sanctuary is not the place for an active barking dog. Nevertheless, birds are far from as likely to become frightened, suspicious, and uneasy when feeding, bathing, singing, and doing other things as when nesting.

Consequently, the time when one must be most careful is during the nesting season. Then it is a good plan to have it quiet in the sanctuary and to keep away from nests whenever possible. Many birds desert their nests if they believe their whereabouts known to others. I often hurry off the moment I discover a new nest without stopping to take a good look at it. And, when I pass it afterwards, I walk by at a distance and casually glance that way in order to see how things are getting along. If you pass a nest at a distance without stopping, and pass it again and again, the birds soon get used to you and are not afraid. Nests should not be visited many times a day, day after day. After the birds have been sitting on their nests for a long time, and the eggs are about to hatch, one can go nearer to them without causing the owners to desert them. But even then one cannot be too careful.

Birds do not desert their nests after they hold youngsters, so a judicious visit is not likely to cause any trouble. But there are other reasons why one should visit such nests as little as possible and not go too near them. Many wild animals follow our footsteps by means of the power of scent and thus find the nests we visit. Then, too, young birds are tender and quickly suffer if exposed to the cold, or

This young cedar waxwing took berries from our fingers.

the hot rays of the sun, or are not fed regularly. The larger the young birds are, however, the less likely they are to be harmed by exposure or lack of food.

Wild animals of many kinds prey upon birds, devouring many eggs and nestlings and sometimes catching an adult bird for good measure. It is during the nesting season that they destroy the most adult birds, because they are then able to pounce upon ground-nesting species while they are incubating their eggs and brooding their young. There are few wild animals, with the exception perhaps of the porcupine, woodchuck, and muskrat, that do not occasionally dine upon adult birds, their eggs and young. Wild animals that live mainly on insects, mice, and other animal foods destroy birds whenever they get the chance. Foxes, weasels, minks, skunks, and red squirrels devour many eggs and birds each year. Still, few people who are interested in attracting birds to the yard are likely to have a great deal of trouble because of the depredations of wild animals. Squirrels, especially red squirrels, are most likely to prove annoying, although a stray weasel may decide to take up lodgings near you in order to secure an easy living on what it is able to find in the neighborhood. The best way to get rid of wild-animal pests, if there are any about, is to shoot or trap them. Although I live on a farm I have never been troubled by wild animals of any kind. I have never found it necessary to shoot and trap them to protect our birds; and, if some animal did begin preying upon them, I should make it a point to kill the guilty animal only, not every one I was able to catch or shoot.

Birds are among the worst enemies of other birds, in fact Burroughs goes so far as to say they are the worst. Shrikes, or butcher birds, often kill small songbirds, storing them in the crotches of trees, behind splinters, and in cracks and crevices for future use. Sometimes they impale their little victims on thorns or the barbs of wires. But butcher birds also kill many insects, mice, and English sparrows and thus do more good than harm; so, unless they actually live in your neighborhood and regularly prey upon small songbirds, they should be left alone.

Some hawks prey upon smaller birds. Others do much more good than harm, catching and devouring rats, mice, gophers, moles, shrews, grasshoppers, crickets, centipedes, millipedes, beetles, and so on, and therefore should not be molested. We have but

The sparrow hawk is a very useful bird as it destroys many mice and grasshoppers.

two common destructive hawks, the Cooper and sharp-shinned hawks. I have already told of how a goshawk killed a bobwhite in the pasture, and a sharp-shinned hawk killed a junco near the barn. The goshawk, too, is a very destructive hawk, killing and eating many rabbits, squirrels, grouse, and bobwhites. But this hawk is rare in the United States, since it nests in Canada and only comes as far south as our country during hard winters. But when one does come and begins to prey upon birds, it can and will do a great deal of harm unless it is trapped or shot. It will remain in one neighborhood for a long time and catch and kill one bobwhite after another, and also other birds, until few of them are left. These hawks sometimes may be caught in traps set on the tops of stubs, posts, and poles, which are their favorite perching places. Or they may be stalked and shot.

The goshawk, Cooper, and sharp-shinned hawks are known as blue darters because of their bluish plumage and swift, darting flight which enables them to pounce upon and catch birds and other prey. The goshawk is a large fellow nearly two feet in length, and it is fierce, blood-thirsty, and destructive. Fortunately it is rare and consequently not likely to molest your feathered neighbors. But the Cooper and sharp-shinned are more numerous and should be known and guarded against. The best way to identify these birds is by their bluish plumage, long tails, slender bodies, short wings, and comparatively small size.

The Cooper hawk is sixteen inches in length, while the sharp-shinned is but twelve, being little larger than a blue jay. It is the more destructive of the two and has the end of its long tail rounded, while the sharp-shinned hawk's is more square at the corners. We have another blue or grayish hawk that has a long tail, the marsh hawk, which is very useful, and which should not be destroyed; this bird may be known by its white rump and its habit of sailing near the ground over meadows and marshes.

Our other common hawks, the sparrow hawk, broad-winged hawk, red-shouldered hawk, red-tailed hawk, and rough-legged hawk are useful and should not be killed. The sparrow hawk is very small, being only about ten inches in length; it often uses an old flicker's hole for nesting purposes. This hawk destroys many mice, grasshoppers, and crickets and is also known as the killy hawk, because *"kil-ly, kil-ly"* is what it seems to say. The broad-winged hawk is about as large as the Cooper hawk, but may be distinguished from the latter by its short tail. The red-tailed and red-shouldered hawks are large birds, the former being about twenty-one inches in length and the latter nineteen. The former has a short reddish tail, while the latter has red shoulders. Both are highly useful, but nevertheless are often called hen or chicken hawks and treated accordingly. They are often to be seen sailing or soaring high in the sky on spring and summer days and to be heard screaming when nesting.

The Cooper and sharp-shinned hawks, not the red-tailed and red-shouldered hawks, are our true hen or chicken hawks. Our useful hawks are of service to us mainly because of the rats, mice, moles, gophers, and other small but destructive animals they kill, to a lesser degree because of the insects they eat. Rats and mice are among the worst of all pests, doing millions upon millions of dollars worth of damage yearly; and birds which habitually prey upon them are well worth having. Rats, mice, potato beetles, cutworms, and striped beetles are the worst pests we have to contend with; consequently, when we remember that hawks destroy many of the rodents, we can be thankful that there are at least a few of them left.

There actually is but one owl that does any harm to speak of, and that is the great horned owl. Though some of them, no doubt, at times take smaller birds,

Young red-shou'dered hawks. They are useful and
should not be killed.

they generally need not be feared. Owls are valuable
chiefly for the rodents they destroy. Our hawks and
owls work a day and a night shift, and so give rats
and mice little rest. Since rats, mice, and owls are
nocturnal, one naturally assumes that owls destroy
more of the rodents than the hawks.

The English sparrow is an enemy of other birds
chiefly because it appropriates nesting boxes not intended for their use. To be sure, this bird does considerable harm in other ways also, taking and damag-
ing fruit, eating grains of various kinds, and visiting
the garden and taking peas, lettuce, and other vegetables. Then, too, it is filthy, often roosting about our
houses, in the lofts of barns and sheds, above side-
walks, and in other places where it is not wanted. A
large flock can and will ruin a great deal of hay and
fodder, if it frequents or roosts in the loft of a barn.

Even a few of the birds can cause one considerable extra work and annoyance. On the other hand, English sparrows do some good, by eating and thus destroying a good many insects in summer, and many weed seeds during the autumn, winter, and early spring months.

If the yard is kept free from garbage and the birds are not provided with suitable nesting and roosting places, there usually will not be enough of them about the premises to cause you much trouble. A few of them are worth having, since they are shrewd little birds, full of life, and cheer one by their presence during the long, cold, winter months. Large flocks often gather in certain places because the lofts of barns and sheds are not properly sealed, or are not kept in good repair. If your buildings are kept tightly sealed,* in good repair, nicely painted, and not cluttered with drain pipes and awnings, the English sparrows usually make their homes elsewhere. Vines and evergreens also attract these birds, which is unfortunate, since these plants are most useful in other ways. Boxes and houses made and set up for blue-

---

*I realize that if the gables of barns and other buildings are not left open or provided with suitable holes for the admittance of barn swallows these useful birds will be robbed of nesting places. However, the holes, or other means of admittance to the lofts of barns and sheds, may be left open during the late spring and summer and kept closed the remainder of the year. This will exclude the English sparrows from the buildings during the autumn, winter, and early spring, when they use them most freely, and will keep them from roosting and securing food and shelter there and from doing much damage to hay and fodder. At the same time the swallows will find them open during their breeding season and will be able to nest there if they so desire.

Eggs of cowbird in the cradle of a field sparrow. The smaller
eggs are those of the field sparrow.

birds, martins, and other birds should be watched
carefully, and English sparrows driven from them
and kept from nesting in them if possible.

If English sparrows are to be found about your
home and sanctuary in large numbers, they may be
trapped, poisoned, or shot. A good way to "shoo"
them is to shoot into the flock a few times with a
shotgun. But they should be shot at only when there
are few other birds about, since shooting frightens
your more desirable bird neighbors also. I have never
found it necessary to trap and poison English sparrows, and have shot but few of them, finding that I
can keep them from haunting the premises in too
large numbers by keeping my buildings closed and
in repair, by keeping the yard free from garbage,
and by dispensing with drain pipes, awnings, dilap-

idated buildings, and other things which attract them. I have always had a few of them about and have treated them much like our other bird neighbors. However, this is a book on attracting birds, not on the control of certain species, so I shall say no more on the matter here. If English sparrows are numerous in your neighborhood, and if they are pests and you feel obliged to get rid of them, send for Farmers' Bulletin No. 493, *The English Sparrow as a Pest*, issued by the United States Department of Agriculture, Washington, D. C., which gives very full directions for trapping, shooting, and poisoning them.*

The cowbird also is an enemy of other birds, laying its eggs in their nests, often removing the rightful eggs to make room for its own, and paying no further attention to them. The young cowbirds hatched from the eggs grow rapidly, often secure more than their share of the food, and crowd the rightful occupants from the nest. Cowbirds lay their eggs in the nests of warblers, field, chipping, vesper, song, and lark sparrows, catbirds, brown thrashers, meadowlarks, thrushes, and so on through a long list.

Birds protect themselves in at least four ways from the impositions of cowbirds: (1) They drive them away from their nests whenever possible; large and aggressive birds are especially likely to do this; (2) They remove and destroy the runt eggs they find in their nests. The two birds I have known to do this are the catbird and brown thrasher; (3) They desert their nests after they have been visited by these

*Or, see *Nature Study and Life*, by C. F. Hodge, pp. 313–317.

Young cowbirds.

birds, leaving the cowbirds' eggs to their fate; field and chipping sparrows often do this; and (4) They build additions to their nests and bury the hateful eggs in the lower part or parts. Yellow warblers protect themselves in this way, building two-, three-, and even four-story nests and thus getting rid of one, two, or more cowbirds' eggs.

Cowbirds are more or less useful because of their feeding habits, eating and destroying many insects and weed seeds. I have never known them to do any harm when feeding, since they never take berries or other fruit, or do any damage in gardens and fields. No doubt some of their food is neutral, being neither of value nor harm to us. Some writers claim that every cowbird to be seen was reared at the expense of three to five pretty and useful birds, but this I believe to be an exaggeration. And some writers think that these birds should be exterminated. I believe that they should be left alone and allowed to destroy all the insects and weed seeds they possibly can. It is rather easy to protect more desirable birds from the impositions of cowbirds. The best way to do this is to remove their eggs with small twigs, when you find them in the nests of more desirable birds. I have removed many cowbirds' eggs from the cradles of other birds and have thus saved the owners and their young a great deal of annoyance — even saved the lives of many pretty songsters. Cowbirds have speckled eggs and these may easily be distinguished from those of birds with blue or pure-white ones. They also are quite unlike the eggs of brown thrashers, and larger than the speckled eggs of sparrows and warblers.

Thousands upon thousands of nests and young birds are lost yearly in fires and through the plowing, cutting over, and pasturing of fields, meadows, and other places. Often a piece of land is allowed to lie idle until the grass gets a good start and then used for a pasture. In the meantime many birds build their nests in such places; and the cattle step on these and destroy them. A big herd of cattle will strip a large field of most of its vegetation in a short time and destroy most of the nests hidden in it. If the cattle were turned in early in the season, or after the birds are through nesting, many broods might be saved. Early plowing also saves many nests. If a piece of land, say a garden or a field, is plowed late in the season, it will be plowed at a time when many birds are nesting there, and the nests will be destroyed. If this had been plowed earlier, the nests might have been saved, since the birds most likely would have built them elsewhere. And the less burning one does the better, since fires not only destroy nests, if they occur during the nesting season, but rob the birds of nesting sites, destroying the dry grass, small bushes, green grass, and even trees. Meadows and hayfields should, if possible, be cut after the nesting season, since thousands of birds nest in hayfields and lose their eggs and young when the hay is cut. To be sure, all the above facts are not applicable to many sanctuaries, but they are to others, and the person interested in the birds should be aware of them and govern his actions accordingly.

A corner of our sanctuary — looking toward the northwest.

Chapter XII

OUR BIRD SANCTUARY

THE first thing we did when we decided to attract
birds to the premises was to set off about an acre
and a half of ground about the house for a wild-life
park or bird sanctuary. We ran our fences in such
a way that this plot of ground could not be used as
a pasture for our cattle and horses. To have a sanctuary worthy of the name, and to attract birds in the
largest numbers you must have many bushes, some
underbrush, vines, grass, wild flowers, and other plants
growing about it. So you cannot afford to pasture

134

the land, since cattle and horses not only eat the grass, but also the leaves of the trees and bushes, and keep many plants from getting a start at all. We also decided to do no burning about our wild-life park, because fires destroy wild flowers, bushes, vines, and trees as effectually as cattle, sheep, and goats. Then, too, we decided to discourage all hunting and the picking of wild flowers. Instead, we aimed to encourage the growth of all trees, bushes, vines, herbs, grasses, wild flowers, and even a few of the more attractive and easily controlled weeds.

There were few wild flowers to be found in our sanctuary at first, because we live in the outskirts of a small city, where most of them had been exterminated before we arrived upon the scene. There was a grove in the northwest corner of our one and one-half acres, all the trees being black and bur oaks, and there were a few stray dewberry, black raspberry, and blackberry vines. There also were a few bird's-foot violets, a single cluster of pasque flowers, some goldenrod, asters, Solomon's seals, and false spikenards, also many dead trees, brush piles, and weeds, such as milkweeds, black nightshade, Canada thistles, and others. There were also a few young trees.

The results of our no-burning, no-pasturing, no-hunting, and no-picking policy were remarkable. The dewberries, blackberries, and black raspberries at once began to spread and now are to be found in all parts of the sanctuary. Of the three we like the wild black raspberries by far the best. We have one large dense thicket of these bushes directly in front of the house and several smaller ones to the north. There now are hundreds of these plants and all of them have sprung from a few stray plants without any work on our part. We just let them alone and allowed them to grow and spread in their own way. Not only are wild black-raspberry bushes very attractive with arched, plumelike canes but they produce a large amount of berries, so many that we sell and can many quarts yearly in addition to what we eat when they are in season and what the birds get away with. The dewberries have spread and multiplied and created two dense clusters about sixteen feet in diameter, while the blackberries have formed three distinct thickets.

There now are hundreds of young trees where there formerly were few or none. Each year dozens of new seedling oaks make their appearance. The first ones to start are now handsome young trees seven or eight feet tall, though others are smaller, ranging in height from one to four feet. The bird's-foot violets now make a creditable showing; the pasque flowers are slowly but surely increasing in numbers, and Solomon's seals and wild spikenards line the sides of the drive by the hundreds. Plants of many other species are now to be found in our sanctuary in numbers: catnip, goldenrod, asters of several species, everlastings, lead plants, wild roses, wild bergamots, pentstemons, and others. Several black-cherry trees have made their appearance, the first one now being of good size, healthy and shapely. No doubt the birds themselves dropped the seeds from which these attractive trees grew, and which we are now using to attract them. Occasionally, too, a tiny evergreen is to be found beneath the oaks. Willows, tiny box elders, sumacs with stout, hairy twigs, elders with lovely clusters of white blossoms, poplars, and hazelnut bushes all grow thrivingly.

Most of the trees, bushes, vines, wild flowers, and other plants now to be found in our bird sanctuary have gained a foothold there without our planting them. But nevertheless, we have planted a variety of things, in fact most anything we have been able to get hold of, our aim being to add attractive wild flowers, trees of various species, bushes and vines, and have them make up thickets.

Among the wild flowers we have planted there are the shooting star, yellow violet, two or three species of blue violets, rue and wood anemones, Dutchman's breeches, spiderwort, Jack-in-the-pulpit, yellow lady's slipper, gill-over-the-ground or ground ivy, wild cranesbill and nodding trillium. We have planted but two vines, the wild grape and the Virginia creeper. The berry or fruit trees we have tried are the Russian mulberry, Juneberry, and the wild choke, black, and red or bird cherries.

We have planted, in the largest numbers, box elders, which we found in the fields, grove, and pasture, springing up here and there and everywhere as tiny seedlings. They are so easy to make grow, and we were so anxious to get all the trees we could, that for many years we transplanted all we found. Now this is no longer a necessity; instead we are obliged at times to rigidly prune and destroy some.

These humble trees have done their part nobly,

Looking toward the east.

enabling us to have many feathered friends, guests, and neighbors we otherwise might not have had, and made our place more attractive to us as well as the birds. We planted large numbers of these trees solely because they are easy to make grow and grow rapidly. And, naturally enough, we shall always feel grateful to the box elder for the excellent service it has rendered. We also planted many cottonwoods, which are easy to start and grow several feet each year. American elms we planted by the score, most of them as tiny seedlings; some of these now are twenty feet tall, about as large as the box elders but somewhat smaller than the cottonwoods. Then, too, we planted several canoe birches, which are easier to grow than we thought. Hardy catalpas, black walnuts, junipers, other evergreens, lindens, wild crab apples, locust, ash trees and wild plums were scattered here and there. We also have a few peach and apple trees.

Although we established our sanctuary mainly for the birds, several other wild creatures make their home in it throughout the year. Several gray squirrels live either in or near it and are to be seen there daily, now on the ground hunting acorns, now running up and down the trunks of the trees, and now scampering leisurely or hurriedly over the snow, or traveling from place to place by means of branch roads. Each year several new squirrels' nests are built about the tops of the oaks, in which the frisky, acrobatic animals rear their young and spend much of their time in the winter. Flying squirrels often make their home in the grove, invariably living in the old holes in oak trees made by woodpeckers, from which I sometimes frighten them by tapping on the trunk with a stick. The timid, sleepy little animals come scampering forth, watch me with large, dreamy eyes, but soon return to their snug nests within the trees.

White-footed, deer, or wood mice, handsome little rodents which resemble flying squirrels in being nocturnal, and in having white underparts and large eyes, also live in the grove and thickets.

The cottontail rabbits, next to the gray squirrels, make the most use of our little sanctuary, some of them living there all year long. They visit our thickets, scamper about the bushes, elude dogs by taking refuge beneath the porch, and live on various

Nooks such as this attract many, many birds in the
course of a year.

things they find in the neighborhood, such as grass,
hay, weeds, bark, twigs, shoots, and stray vegetables.
In winter we find their tracks or trails in the snow,
and in summer we see many youngsters, who spend
most of their time in the grass and thickets, but who
sometimes come forth from their hiding places toward night and feast on the clover found near the
edge of the lawn.

The house cat is one of the worst enemies of birds,
and this problem we have solved very satisfactorily
by not having one. To be sure, stray ones occasionally come our way, but we have never found it necessary to kill or persecute them. Most of them seem to
come to the neighborhood for the purpose of hunting mice and rats about the garden, fields, corn

shocks, hay stack, barn, shed, and henhouse. We do not keep a dog for the same reason that we keep no cat. Dogs, as a rule, do not harm birds, although they sometimes frighten them; and, of course, if we had one, he might chase and otherwise make life miserable for the squirrels and cottontails.

Cats and birds make a poor combination, and it seems to me it is inconsistent to keep a cat and have a bird sanctuary, since the natural tendency of the cat is to kill and frighten the birds you are trying to help and attract. Your cat may be the best cat in the world, and may never have harmed a bird, but the birds are not likely to trust her. A cat, whether she be good or just the reverse, is perhaps as good a scarecrow, or "scarebird" (if I may invent a term) as you can keep about the premises. However, if you decide to attract birds and keep a cat, feed her well and see that she stays where she can be of service catching mice, or at least where she can do no harm, preferably in the barn, granary, or shed, and do not allow her to roam wherever her fancy and appetite lead her. And since cats do more damage when the birds are nesting than at other times, they should then be confined or watched very carefully.

"But," you say, "my neighbors all have cats that are likely to prey, or do prey, upon my birds; what shall I do about it?" In the first place, if a stray cat visits your sanctuary, you may kill it if you so desire. Or, you may protect your tree-nesting birds by placing tin or sheet-iron guards about the trunks of the trees. If a wide piece of tin or sheet iron is wrapped around the trunk and secured with a small nail or

A quintet of fine young blue jays.

two, this alone will keep a cat from climbing that particular tree and robbing the nests located in it. Or, the lower half of a piece of tin or sheet iron may be cut into strips and the strips bent outward and an excellent guard thus made. Food trays, birdbaths, and nesting boxes fastened to poles, posts, and trees also may be protected in this way, if cats are likely to visit them and kill or frighten your birds. And lastly, you can always talk the matter over with your neighbors and try to secure their co-operation. Most people love birds and will meet you halfway if you approach them in the right way.

Some folks find it necessary to persecute different forms of animal life in order to encourage others, shooting one species of bird and helping another, killing cats and feeding birds, and warring on crows, blackbirds, English sparrows, and cowbirds and attracting chickadees, nuthatches, and juncos, but the writer has never found it necessary to do much persecuting. I do not hate cats, dogs, English sparrows, cowbirds, and crows, and I have never found it necessary to kill many of them. Although I do not keep a cat, I do not dislike cats, rather I am fond of them, and dogs too, and am only following a plan I find works out rather well for both cats and birds. Furthermore, in order to attract, help, and protect birds it is hardly necessary to antagonize your neighbors by shooting their pets. If you are cheerful, enthusiastic, and friendly, you are quite likely to get their good will, co-operation, and interest in your bird-conservation efforts.

Children also sometimes prove a problem to the bird landlord and bird lover. Some of them rob the nests of birds, others shoot many of them, and still others cause them to desert their nests. Children, naturally, should be reminded that it is cruel and wrong to injure birds, rob their nests, shoot them, and cause them to desert their nests. The best way to avoid trouble with children is to interest them in birds and to impress upon them the fact that birds are useful. Children who are interested in birds and who enjoy hearing, seeing, watching, and studying them do not injure them. Those who are interested in making and setting out birdbaths, food trays, and nesting boxes are not likely to rob the nests of birds or to do anything which injures or frightens them. The boy who is interested in bird study and who is doing what he can to help and attract birds is not likely to hunt them with a slingshot, air gun, or rifle.

Interest in and enthusiasm for bird study and means of attracting birds is more or less infectious. If you are interested in the birds and are doing what you can to help, protect, and attract them, others will become interested and will be likely to do what you are doing. The thing spreads and grows until the whole neighborhood is more or less interested and most of your problems thereby most satisfactorily solved.

INDEX